THE WORLD OF THE END

How Jesus' Prophecy Shapes Our Priorities

STUDY GUIDE | NINE LESSONS

DR. DAVID JEREMIAH

HarperChristian
Resources

The World of the End Study Guide
© 2022 by Dr. David P. Jeremiah
P.O. Box 3838, San Diego, CA 92163

Requests for information should be addressed to:
HarperChristian Resources, 3900 Sparks Dr. SE, Grand Rapids, Michigan 49546

ISBN 978-0-310-15592-8 (softcover)
ISBN 978-0-310-15593-5 (ebook)

HarperChristian Resources titles may be purchased in bulk for church, business, fundraising, or ministry use. For information, please e-mail ResourceSpecialist@ChurchSource.com.

Edited by Jordan Davis.

Published in association with Yates & Yates, www.yates2.com.

First Printing November 2022 / Printed in the United States of America

CONTENTS

HOW TO USE
THIS STUDY GUIDE

The purpose of this study guide is to reinforce Dr. David Jeremiah's dynamic, in-depth teaching and to aid you in applying biblical truth to your daily life. This study guide is designed to be used in conjunction with *The World of the End* by Dr. David Jeremiah, but it may also be used by itself for personal or group study.

Structure of the Lessons

Each lesson is based on the corresponding chapter in *The World of the End* and focuses on specific passages in the Bible. Each lesson is composed of the following elements:

- **Outline:** The outline at the beginning of the lesson gives a clear, concise picture of the topic being studied and will provide a helpful framework for you as you go through Dr. Jeremiah's teaching or read the book.

- **Overview:** The overview summarizes Dr. Jeremiah's teaching on the passage being studied in the lesson. You should refer to the Scripture passages in your own Bible as you study the overview. Unless otherwise indicated, Scripture verses quoted are taken from the *New King James Version*.

- **Application:** This section contains a variety of individual and group discussion questions designed to help you dig deeper into the lesson and the Scriptures and to apply the lesson to your daily life. For Bible study groups or Sunday school classes, these questions will provide a springboard for group discussion and interaction.

- **Did You Know?** This section presents a fascinating fact, historical note, or insight that adds a point of interest to the preceding lesson.

Personal Study

The lessons in *The World of the End Study Guide* were created to help you gain fresh insights into God's Word and to develop new perspectives on topics that you may have previously studied. Each lesson is designed to challenge your thinking and help you grow in your knowledge of Christ. During your study, it is our prayer that you will discover how biblical truth affects every aspect of your life and your relationship with Christ will be strengthened.

When you commit to completing this study guide, try to set apart a time, daily or weekly, to read through the lessons without distraction. Have your Bible nearby when you read the study guide, so you're ready to look up verses if you need to. If you want to use a notebook to write down your thoughts, be sure to have that handy as well. Take your time to think through and answer the questions. If you plan on reading the study guide with a small group, be sure to read ahead and be prepared to take part in the weekly discussions.

Group Study

The lessons in this study guide are suitable for Sunday school classes, small-group studies, elective Bible studies, or home Bible study groups. Each person in the group should have his or her own study guide. You may wish to complete the study guide lesson as homework prior to the meeting of the group and then use the meeting time to discuss the lesson. If you are a group leader, refer to the guide at the back of this book for additional instructions on how to set up and lead your group time.

For Continuing Study

For a complete listing of Dr. Jeremiah's materials for personal and group study, call 1-800-947-1993, go online to www.DavidJeremiah.org, or write to Turning Point, P.O. Box 3838, San Diego, CA 92163.

Dr. Jeremiah's *Turning Point* program is currently heard or viewed around the world on radio, television, and the Internet in English. *Momento Decisivo*, the Spanish translation of Dr. Jeremiah's messages, can be heard on radio in every Spanish speaking country in the world. The television broadcast is also broadcast by satellite throughout the Middle East with Arabic subtitles.

Contact Turning Point for radio and television program times and stations in your area, or visit our website at www.DavidJeremiah.org/stationlocator.

THE WORLD OF THE END

When we think of Jesus, the mental setting that we place Him is invariably in large crowds—and rightfully so. On many occasions, Jesus preached to crowds numbering into the tens of thousands. This includes the Sermon on the Mount where He used the reverberation of the hillside to speak to the thousands sitting in the valley below.

Remember that the woman who touched the hem of Jesus' garment that she might be healed was in a crowd so large that He did not see her. One group of men lowered their friend from the roof of a house to get access to Jesus because so many people were present. And many people were there for His first miracle at the wedding in Cana. The biblical account does not make it seem like a small affair.

Therefore, it is safe to say that Jesus was used to being in large crowds. And yet two significant moments in Jesus' life described in the Bible had audiences of less than five people. The Transfiguration when Jesus met with Moses and Elijah on a high mountain was witnessed by only Peter, James, and John. And Jesus' greatest prophetic sermon, the Olivet Discourse, was heard and attended by only four men: Peter, James, John, and Andrew.

This seemingly private conversation between Jesus and His closest disciples was actually a detailed preview into what the Last Days on earth would look like before His Second Coming. Sitting high on the Mount of Olives overlooking the holy city of Jerusalem, Jesus first predicted the destruction of the temple that would incredibly happen only years later in AD 70. He did this to give credence to His other prophecies. However, the prophecy He followed with detailed what the World of the End would look like.

So often when the subject of end-times prophecy comes up, Christian believers turn to the books of Daniel and Revelation. And while these books are the source of great material and information, too often the Olivet Discourse of Jesus is ignored when it comes to studying the end of days. But wouldn't it make sense to heed the words of not only the Author of Creation, but the very One who will herald the end of time with His swift coming?

This study guide, *The World of the End*, seeks to rectify that hole in our knowledge and to focus specifically and intentionally on Jesus' prophecy in Matthew 24:1–14. Jesus makes it clear that all the signs He points to won't occur at once; instead, they will gradually appear and become stronger and more frequent as the World of the End draws near.

In the pages ahead, we will look at Jesus' prophetic warning about what life will be like on the earth in the World of the End. There will be wars and rumors of wars. There will be deceivers, both within and without the Church. Natural disasters will cause great damage and death throughout the world. And the rule of law will concede into utter anarchy.

However, amid all that bad news, Jesus does not leave us without hope! Within this passage of Scripture, He gives us ways to combat all the surmounting evil that Christians will face. Jesus enables us and points us to tools that will allow us to endure with truth, love, and faith until the very day of His coming. So be prepared to learn what is coming and what you can do to make a determined stand for Christ in the World of the End.

THE PROPHECY

MATTHEW 24:1–3

In this lesson we are introduced to the Olivet Discourse.

There is an inherent and insatiable human appetite for knowing what the future holds. Whether it is economic forecasts or the ever-shifting geopolitical environments around the world, everyone wants to have a sense for what is coming. And there is no shortage of modern-day prophets who claim to see what lies ahead. But in the Bible, there is an oft-ignored passage of Scripture where Jesus, the Son of God Himself, delineates once and for all what will truly come to pass at the end of days.

OUTLINE

   I. **The Setting of the Prophecy**

  II. **The Subject of the Prophecy**
     A. The Profound Prediction
     B. The Precise Performance

 III. **The Secret to the Prophecy**

IV. **The Scope of the Prophecy**

V. **The Significance of the Prophecy**
   A. Jesus Wants to Teach Us About the Future
   B. Jesus Wants to Transform Us for the Future
   C. Jesus Wants Us to Trust Him with the Future

OVERVIEW

During a 2007 interview with *USA Today*, Microsoft CEO Steve Ballmer made a shockingly inaccurate prediction. He told reporter David Lieberman, "There's no chance that the iPhone is going to get any significant market share." Ballmer seemed to base his prediction on the notion that iPhones would be interesting to technology aficionados, but not to the overall general population. Fifteen years later with more than two billion iPhones sold, it's safe to say that Steve Ballmer was wrong.[1]

Our world is filled with a plethora of people who make predictions. Prognosticators and prediction makers are always able, willing, and ready to share their opinions. In fact, today there are approximately two million podcasters, 600,000 journalists, and nearly 400 twenty-four-hour news networks. Plus, there are countless ministers filling the pulpits each Sunday. All of them are vying for your attention so that they can tell you what is going on now and what will happen in the future.

We hear so many voices, arguments, and speculations on a daily basis that it is literally overwhelming to determine what is true. Everybody has a theory and a slant that they seek to share. How are we to weed through all those outlets and determine what is true? Who has the right take on the future?

I would like to suggest to you that there is one opinion we ought to value more than all the other opinions combined. Amid the thousands of shrill voices that are being heard today, we need to listen to One Voice—the voice of the Lord Jesus Christ.

But what does Jesus have to say about the future that we face? It may surprise you to discover that one of Jesus' longest messages in the New Testament is all about the future. In the Gospels of Matthew, Mark, and

Luke, there is a section referred to as "The Olivet Discourse." This title is derived from the location of its delivery; Jesus answered the questions of His disciples while sitting on the Mount of Olives (see Mark 13:3).

The message that Jesus delivered to His disciples on that historic day is the second longest message of Jesus recorded in the Bible. The only one longer is the Sermon on the Mount (see Matthew 5–7), but that was a public message given at the beginning of His ministry. The Olivet Discourse was a private message given at the end of Jesus' ministry to just four of His disciples.[2]

The late pastor and author Tim LaHaye was a lover of the Olivet Discourse. He wrote this description of it in one of his books:

> The Olivet Discourse, delivered shortly before Jesus' crucifixion, is the most important single passage of prophecy in all the Bible. It is significant because it came from Jesus Himself immediately after He was rejected by His own people and because it provides the master outline of end-time events.[3]

The Setting of the Prophecy

In order to properly process and understand the Olivet Discourse, we need to grasp its setting in the life of Christ. In Matthew 24:1 we read, "Then Jesus went out and departed from the temple, and His disciples came up to show Him the buildings of the temple."

To put our Lord's great prophecy in its proper context, we must feel the gravity of the moment. This event didn't just happen in a vacuum of time. This happened during Passover week, which turned out to be the last week of Jesus' life before He went to the cross.

That final week of Jesus' life must have been a disappointment to Him. It was during that week that He cleansed the temple from those who were merchandising and ripping off the Jewish people in the Name of God. It was also within this week when He famously walked by a fig tree that wasn't bearing any fruit and cursed it, declaring it would never bear fruit again, illustrating that if you claim to be something, it should be evident in your life. Theologian John Walvoord said this about those final days of Jesus' life:

As Christ dealt with spiritual, theological, and moral apostasy in His day in Matthew 23, He delivered the most scathing denunciation of false religion and hypocrisy to be found anywhere. He calls the scribes and the Pharisees hypocrites no less than seven times (Matthew 23:13, 14, 15, 23, 25, 27, 29). He calls them blind five times (23:16, 17, 19, 24, 26), labels them fools twice (23:17, 19), describes them as whited sepulchers (23:27), serpents or snakes, the children of poisonous vipers (23:33), and declares that they are in danger of going to hell. It would be difficult to find words more biting than these words of Christ used to characterize the religion of His day.[4]

And while the righteous anger of Jesus was expressed in His fiery words against these people, the fact is—though He was very angry at their conduct—He loved them! These were His people, and He was heartbroken over having to leave the temple and the chosen people which should have received Him, but did not.

It is directly out of this environment and attitude that Jesus is about to give the Olivet Discourse to His disciples. In this context, He will speak as a prophet. He will accurately forecast the future of the Jewish people as well as predict some things that will affect you and me. And you can count on it that when Jesus says something will happen, it will happen.

The Subject of the Prophecy

In Matthew 24:2–3, Jesus lays out the specifics of His prophecy.

> And Jesus said to them, "Do you not see all these things? Assuredly, I say to you, not one stone shall be left here upon another, that shall not be thrown down." Now as He sat on the Mount of Olives, the disciples came to Him privately, saying, "Tell us, when will these things be? And what will be the sign of Your coming, and of the end of the age?"

Jesus responds to the disciples' awe of the physical stature of the temple by sitting down with them on the Mount of Olives. In that culture, sitting down was the posture a teacher would take before he was to give an important lesson. This is the final teaching recorded for us in the book of Matthew, and it is also Jesus' most important lesson on the World of the End and what it will be like when that time comes.

From the Mount of Olives, Jesus and His disciples had a staggering view of Jerusalem and the temple complex. It was at this place and in this moment that Jesus uttered this unbelievable prophecy—that the temple was going to be destroyed.

The Profound Prediction

Jesus pointed to the temple and said to the disciples, "Do you not see all these things? Assuredly, I say to you, not one stone shall be left here upon another, that shall not be thrown down" (Matthew 24:2). What was Jesus doing when He made that prediction? He was about to file His credentials as a prophet.

The Old Testament says a prophet is known by whether what he prophesies comes true. And if it doesn't come true, he is a false prophet. You don't pass as a prophet with an eighty or ninety percent accuracy rate; you must be one hundred percent accurate all the time.

When Jesus said that the temple complex would be flattened and would never appear again in the same way, the disciples must have thought that was an absurd statement. Herod's temple complex was one of the wonders of the ancient world and a source of tremendous pride for the Jews. The ancient historian Josephus wrote about the temple, "The most admirable of all the works that we have seen or heard of, both for its curious structure and its magnitude, and also for the vast wealth bestowed upon it, as well as for the glorious reputation it had for its holiness."[5]

The temple was one of the most expansive, majestic, and important buildings in all the world. But Jesus said unequivocally that it was all going down. You must wonder what was going through the minds of the disciples when they heard His words.

The Precise Performance

In AD 70, the Roman general Titus built wooden scaffolds around the walls of the temple buildings—a tactic with no previous use recorded. He piled the scaffolds high with wood and other flammable items and set them all on fire. The heat from the fires grew so intense that the temple structure was weakened, allowing the Romans to dislodge the giant stones from one another, prying them off one by one.

Soldiers then sifted through the rubble that was left on the temple site trying to find any of the gold that had melted into the ruins. The site of the temple complex was absolutely flattened—exactly as Jesus had said.[6]

After Jesus' prediction, the temple was destroyed, and today the location is a walled compound within the Old City of Jerusalem. It is the site of the Dome of the Rock to the north and the Al-Aqsa Mosque to the south. In the southwest stands the Western Wall—the retaining wall of Herod's Temple Mount and the lone testimony to a once grand site.

Because the prophecy and the fulfillment of the temple destruction has already happened, we are able to verify the accuracy of Jesus' words. We see that what He said would occur happened just as He said it would, down to the very last stone. What then should we think about the things He has predicted that are yet to be fulfilled? We should have every confidence that they will happen with the very precision He used in describing the destruction of the temple.

In fact, after He predicts the destruction of the temple in Matthew 24, Jesus lays out in vivid detail what events will happen in real time before He returns. Here is a synopsis of those future signs of His coming.

Matt 24:

- There will be deception by false christs (see verses 4–5).
- There will be dissention between the nations of the world (see verses 6–7).
- There will be devastation worldwide (see verses 7–8).
- There will be deliverance of believers to tribulation (see verse 9).
- There will be defection of false believers (see verses 10–13).
- There will be declaration of the Gospel to the whole world (see verse 14).

Do any of those progressions look familiar to you? Are any of them happening today? Once again, Jesus' accuracy in describing the destruction of the temple allows us to have full faith and confidence that when He describes the signs of the end of the age, they will surely come to pass.

The Secret to the Prophecy

To help us understand how these predictions will unfold, Jesus employs a graphic picture and one that may have special significance to many women: Jesus says that the events of Matthew 24 are the "beginning of birth pains" (verse 8 NIV).

A woman may feel one such pain then not feel another for twenty minutes or more, but as birth approaches, the pains become more intense, and the timing of the pains becomes closer together. When you reach a stage where the pain is very intense and those pains are gripping you with regular frequency, you know you'd better get to the hospital or you're going to give birth in the backseat of the car!

It is interesting to note that in one of his letters to the Thessalonians, Paul uses the very same illustration that Jesus used here. Paul says that the return of Christ will come as a thief in the night—unexpectedly, quietly, and suddenly. Look at his words from 1 Thessalonians 5:

> But concerning the times and the seasons, brethren, you have no need that I should write to you. For you yourselves know perfectly that the day of the Lord so comes as a thief in the night. For when they say, "Peace and safety!" then sudden destruction comes upon them, as labor pains upon a pregnant woman. And they shall not escape (verses 1–3).

Jesus and Paul are both reiterating that when you see the first signs of His coming, it will be like childbirth—it won't be immediate, but it won't be long either! As we study this section of the Olivet Discourse, keep in mind that the things that are going to happen in the future will not all occur at one time. They will be like birth pains with the frequency and intensity of each gradually increasing. And the rate and concentration of those events in the End Times will only rachet up until the eventual Second Coming of Jesus Christ.

The Scope of the Prophecy

We have limited our study for this series to the first fourteen verses of Matthew 24 because these are the verses that affect us right now. Our

Lord's words directly apply to us at this critical hour of history. These verses describe what life will be like on the earth as we move closer to the time of the Rapture.

But here is the key to our application: If you study Matthew 24 and Revelation 6, Jesus agrees with John, and John agrees with Jesus. They accurately describe the very events in world history that are going to happen.

But these events will not begin to be felt as birth pains after the Rapture, they will begin now! In the days building up to our Lord's return for His own, we will begin to feel the pain of those signs that we're feeling right now.

For instance, one of the signs is to let no one deceive you. Have we ever lived in a day when deceit is so rampant? We live in a time of increasing deceitfulness and an increasing lack of truth.

All the signs that Jesus said would increase as we move toward the end have started. I am not going to predict when Jesus will come back. I don't have the right to do that, and the Bible tells us not to do that. However, we are to be aware of the signs of the times. We need to be aware of what's going on.

The Significance of the Prophecy

What Jesus shared in the Olivet Discourse is not some ivory tower, academic knowledge that has no impact on our lives. The significance of this prophecy is significant and real and can be broken into three ideas.

Jesus Wants to Teach Us About the Future

Are you aware Jesus wants you to know about the future? He was always preparing His disciples for the future. Unless we have a firm grasp on what the Bible teaches us about the future, we cannot properly handle the strains of everyday life. Even when you know what Jesus says about the future, if you're not careful and you watch too much television, you can become really depressed! But as John M. Frame once wrote, "So far as I can see, every Bible passage about the return of Christ is written for a practical purpose—not to help us to develop a theory of history, but to motivate our obedience."[7]

Jesus Wants to Transform Us for the Future

Jesus not only wants to teach us about the future, but He also wants us to be ready for the future. In John 16:1, Jesus said, "These things I have spoken to you, that you should not be made to stumble." The days are coming when the hand of God will move in astounding ways. And if we know the Word of God, we won't be taken by surprise. We will find ourselves not panicked, but excited about what we see the Lord doing as we anticipate His return.

Jesus Wants Us to Trust Him with the Future

Jesus wants to teach us and transform us for the future, but most importantly, He wants us to trust Him with the future. It is interesting to note that Jesus never really answered the disciples' questions fully. For instance, He told them how the temple would be destroyed, but He didn't tell them the exact date. But years later they saw it come to pass exactly as He said it would.

Jesus is not obligated to give us the answers to every single question we ask. What Jesus wants us to do amid all the uncertainty we face today is to learn how to trust Him. And that means learning how to trust Him when it looks like everything is falling apart.

We need to remember that no matter what, Jesus is still on His throne. Nothing catches Him by surprise. He is the Sovereign God, He is in control, and you can trust Him. In the midst of what is happening today and what is going to happen tomorrow, you can trust Jesus.

No one knows what deceight is because no one knows what the truth is.

APPLICATION

Personal Questions

1. Read Mark 13:3.

   a. Which disciples were with Jesus when He gave this message?

   Peter, James, John, Andrew

   b. Where did Jesus deliver the Olivet Discourse?

   Mount of Olives,

the things of the world - the bad - are here to make us better. 19

c. Why do you think Jesus gave this message to only a few disciples?

Closest?

2. Read Matthew 24:1–3.

a. From where did Jesus depart?

temple
"left" the temple, left really —

b. What was the subject of the prophecy that He spoke of?

temple coming down

3. How long did it take for Jesus' prediction to come true?

40 years

4. What now sits on the land where the temple used to be?

Wailing Wall

5. Will the things Jesus predicted happen all at one time? (See the section titled "The Secret to the Prophecy.")

No

6. Based on the three ideas that make up the significance of the prophecy, what was Jesus' intention in His message? List the three ideas below.

Pg 18-19

teach, transform, trust Him with the future

7. No matter what happens, why is it important to remember that Jesus is on His throne?

Believe – no surprises – Jesus is in control

8. Does anything come as a surprise to Him? How does knowing this give you comfort?

no, knowing Jesus is in control

Group Questions

1. Read Matthew 24:1–3 as a group.

   a. What message of Jesus are we introduced to?

   the end of the ages - signs

   b. Why is this message relevant today?

   they are happening today

   c. Together, explain what your first impressions are of this passage.

   Scary? Look toward future

2. Why is it important to understand the setting of this prophecy?

    it happened

    a. At the time, what was going on in the final days of Jesus' life on earth?

    Romans taking over
    Jesus was disappointed — " left the temple"

    b. What festival was being celebrated prior to His death on the cross?

    passover

3. According to Matthew 24:1–2, what were the specifics of Jesus' prophecy?

4. In the Old Testament, what was a prophet known by? Based on Jesus' own prophecy, would we be able to call Him a prophet as well?

5. Because Jesus' prophecy was fulfilled, we can verify the accuracy of His words. Discuss how we should think about the things He has spoken, but are yet to be fulfilled.

6. Jesus used an illustration to help us understand His predictions (see Matthew 24:8 NIV). What was it?

7. What were the three ideas behind the significance of the prophecy? Discuss each one in detail with the group.

8. From this lesson, how can you learn to trust Jesus more with your future? Share your answer with the group.

DID YOU KNOW?

The Olivet Discourse is recorded in three places in the Bible: Matthew 24; Mark 13; and Luke 21. The site of its delivery, the Mount of Olives, is a real and significant location both in biblical times and today. This was the very place where Jesus ascended into heaven (see Acts 1:9–12). It is also the same place to which He will one day return (see Acts 1:12; Zechariah 14:4). And even today, it has one of the most breathtaking views in all the world, especially when the morning sun casts its glow across the golden city of Jerusalem with its haunting walls, limestone buildings, and iconic images like the Temple Mount.

Notes

1. Jay Yarow, "Here's What Steve Ballmer Thought About The iPhone Five Years Ago," *Insider*, June 29, 2012, https://www.businessinsider.com/heres-what-steve-ballmer-thought-about-the-iphone-five-years-ago-2012-6?IR=T.

2. John MacArthur, *The Second Coming* (Wheaton, IL: Crossway, 1999), 69.

3. Tim LaHaye and Thomas Ice, *Charting The End Times: A Visual Guide to Understanding Bible Prophecy* (Eugene, OR: Harvest House, 2001), 35.

4. John F. Walvoord, "Christ's Olivet Discourse on the End of the Age," *Bible.org*, accessed May 31, 2022, https://bible.org/seriespage/1-introduction-2.

5. Flavius Josephus, *The Wars of the Jews, 6.267*, accessed July 11, 2022, https://lexundria.com/j_bj/6.267/wst.

6. Flavius Josephus, *The War of the Jews*, https://www.gutenberg.org/files/2850/2850-h/2850-h.htm.

7. John M. Frame, *Systematic Theology: An Introduction to Christian Belief* (Phillipsburg, NJ: P&R Publishing, 2013), 1094.

IN A WORLD OF DECEPTION, BE HONEST

MATTHEW 24:4–5, 11

In this lesson we learn that the only way to fight deceit is to live out the truth with boldness.

The more wicked and twisted and dark the world becomes, the greater impact and force that the singular light of truth will have. And as Christians, we have direct access to the Way, the Truth, and the Life: Jesus Christ.

OUTLINE

I. The Status of Deception in the World of the End

II. The Source of Deception in the World of the End

III. The Strategy of Deception in the World of the End
   A. Satan Disputes God's Word
   B. Satan Denies God's Word
   C. Satan Displaces God's Word
   D. Satan Discounts God's Goodness
   E. Satan Dramatizes God's Restrictions
   F. Satan Diminishes God's Penalty

IV. The Solution to Deception in the World of the End
   A. Tell the Truth
   B. Test the Truth
   C. Teach the Truth

OVERVIEW

In 1989, the Romanian Revolution brought an end to the brutal reign of dictator Nicolae Ceaușescu and his wife, Elena. Their entire story can be wrapped up in one word: deception.

From the very beginning, Ceaușescu's twenty-four-year rule was saturated with falsehood. He deceived the Romanian people when he proposed a utopian vision for their country, promising the end of oppression and the beginning of prosperity. The harsh reality was he delivered an iron hand that crushed his own people and squeezed the nation dry.

But the couple's deception was not limited to Romania or Eastern Europe; they deceived the whole world! Queen Elizabeth II knighted Ceaușescu. The United States government granted his country "most favored nation" trading status. And former Israeli prime minister Menachem Begin credited Ceaușescu with mediating Anwar Sadat's peace mission to Jerusalem.

In actuality, the Ceaușescus were every bit as evil as Hitler; they just didn't have the opportunity to work on as grand a scale. They were—in every sense of the words—liars and master manipulators.

Deception is common practice in our modern world today. But it is also a frequent topic throughout Scripture. While the practice of deceit began in Genesis 3 with the fall of man in the Garden of Eden, it also seems to occupy an especially significant place in the prophetic passages of the New Testament.

When the disciples came to Jesus asking Him about the future (see Matthew 24:3), Jesus began His response with this serious warning: "Take heed that no one deceives you" (Matthew 24:4). Let's take a deeper look and see what this deception Jesus warns us about will look like in the End Times.

The Status of Deception in the World of the End

According to Jesus, deception will play a major role in the World of the End. While we should always be on alert for lies and misdirection from the enemy, the Lord warned us to be especially watchful for spiritual deceit as the day of His return approaches (see Matthew 24:23–24).

In every century since the birth of Christ, there have been imposters who have claimed to be the Messiah. Jesus specifically instructed His disciples not to follow or fall for these false claims. We, too, are to be wary of any such claims and to be vigilant in exposing their falsehood.

But that is not the only deception Jesus cautions us about. In Matthew 24:11, He says, "Then many false prophets will rise up and deceive many." For every one imposter who claims to be the Messiah, there are at least ten false prophets who claim knowledge about the future that they simply cannot know. These are false prophets.

Hundreds of fake religious leaders have predicted the exact date of the Lord's return over the years. Many of these false prophets claimed to base their predictions on their study of the Scripture. But Scripture makes it very clear that the date of our Lord's return is unknown and unknowable by anyone on this earth (see Matthew 24:44; 25:13; Mark 13:32).

Did you know that when Jesus was on this earth, He did not know when He would return? As the Son of God, Jesus was omniscient, but for the time He was on this earth as a man, He voluntarily divested Himself of the independent use of His attributes. Sitting in heaven today, Jesus knows the date of His return, but when He was on this earth, Jesus did not know when He would return. The angels do not even know when He will return.

We should always be ready for the return of Christ, but we should never give dates. Whenever you hear somebody say they know when Jesus is coming back, you can take it to the bank that they are wrong. Scripture clearly says that no man is privy to that information.

The Source of Deception in the World of the End

The spiritual deception that Jesus warns us about isn't mere happenstance. There is someone behind these deceptions, and that someone is none other than Satan—the evil enemy of our souls. He is the father of lies, and since the very beginning of human history, one of his primary weapons against us has been deceit.

In the book of Revelation, John describes him like this: "So the great dragon was cast out, that serpent of old, called the Devil and Satan, who deceives the whole world" (12:9). And in John 8:44, Jesus said this about Satan: "He was a murderer from the beginning, and does not stand in the truth, because there is no truth in him. When he speaks a lie, he speaks from his own resources, for he is a liar and the father of it."

Spiritual deception may be Satan's most insidious weapon against those of us in the Church. That is why Jesus and His apostles speak of it nearly thirty times in the New Testament. Satan is a liar, a serpent, and a deceiver. He always masquerades as something else. As 2 Corinthians 11:14 tells us, "Satan himself transforms himself into an angel of light."

Deception has always been the weapon of choice of our enemy. And when this deception is full-blown in the period surrounding the Rapture, it will be unlike anything that has ever happened before on the earth. However, the birth pangs of deception will be felt throughout the world before the Rapture, and many prophetic scholars believe that they are being felt already today.

What is evident now more than ever is that there is an erosion of trust between the foundations that have held cultures and civilizations together for years. That erosion will only continue to intensify, and we know exactly who is behind it all.

The Strategy of Deception in the World of the End

In 2 Corinthians 2:11, the apostle Paul wrote that we are not to be "ignorant of [Satan's] devices." As followers of Jesus, we need to know our enemy so that we can stand against his schemes. That includes the scheme of deception. Thankfully, we can learn a great deal about Satan's strategy by studying God's Word.

The strategy Satan implemented in the Garden of Eden in Genesis 3 is the exact same strategy he tried to use on Jesus Christ in the wilderness in Matthew 4. And unsurprisingly, it is the same strategy he uses on you and me today.

It is also the same strategy he will use in the End Times. Satan only has one game plan, one strategy. He uses it repeatedly. Let's look at Genesis 3 and find out how Satan works so we can be more prepared not to let him deceive us with his tactics.

Satan Disputes God's Word

The first thing Satan did when he tempted Adam and Eve was to dispute God's Word:

"Has God indeed said, 'You shall not eat of every tree of the garden'?" (Genesis 3:1). Satan immediately tried to water down what God had said and to change it just a little bit. He suggested to Eve that she may not have heard God correctly.

Here is how this happens to us today. We have the clear, plain Word of God in front of us telling us we shouldn't do something we would really like to do. The next thing that happens is that someone sidles up to us and gives us an alternative interpretation of the text that will allow us to do what we know God doesn't want us to do.

That is a moment of decision. We must choose at that moment either to accept the truth of God's Word as it is written or to allow ourselves to be deceived. Satan told Eve that God didn't really mean what He said, and Eve believed him.

Satan Denies God's Word

Next, Satan said to Eve, "You will not surely die" (Genesis 3:4). The road from doubt to denial is clearly not very long, for when Satan said, "You will not surely die," he was brazenly contradicting what God had said. Just look at God's words in Genesis 2:17: "But of the tree of the knowledge of good and evil you shall not eat, for in the day that you eat of it you shall surely die."

It is important to note the sequence here. Doubt opens the door to denial. If Adam and Eve had not listened to Satan in the beginning, they would not have been victimized in the end.

In like fashion, every time you try to find an interpretation of Scripture that will permit you to do something you know is wrong in your heart, you give up a little ground to the enemy. If you keep doing that, eventually you will open the door to Satan, allowing him to deceive you with ease. And he will do it every time.

Satan Displaces God's Word

After Satan disputes God's Word and then denies it, he tells Eve, "You will be like God" (Genesis 3:5). He essentially argues that if you do what God told you not to do, you will be like God.

Satan was simply putting into Eve's mind the same disturbing thought that had once entered his own mind. This was the same impulse that had transformed him from the anointed cherub to the devil of hell.

One of the easiest places to see Satan at work in the world today is to observe how our culture treats sin. For instance, lying doesn't seem so bad if we're trying to spare another person's feelings. Adultery doesn't feel as wrong when we describe it through doublespeak as an "improper relationship." Gluttony and addiction aren't the result of personal choices but are genetic disorders and chemical imbalances.

When we allow Satan to sow doubt in our minds that some sins are really not sins, we open our hearts to his deception. Right and wrong quickly get turned upside down, and God's Word is replaced with our own wisdom. This is how he has always done it.

Satan Discounts God's Goodness

Satan's next tactic is subtle but powerful: He tries to undermine God's goodness and generosity. Note Genesis 2:16–17: "And the Lord God commanded the man, saying, 'Of every tree of the garden you may freely eat; but of the tree of the knowledge of good and evil you shall not eat, for in the day that you eat of it you shall surely die.'"

Did you observe how generous God is? An abundance of goodness was offered freely to Adam, with just one restriction. Yet look at how

Eve reframed God's original command when she spoke with Satan in Genesis 3:2: "We may eat the fruit of the trees of the garden."

Do you see what is missing? Eve omitted God's gracious provision that she and Adam could "freely" eat of every tree in the garden. In other words, her comprehension of God's provision was not nearly as magnanimous as God intended it to be. Satan had gotten to her with his evil implication about God.

When you start to question the goodness of God, you are on the road to deception. Don't allow Satan to push you into thinking that God has not been good to you or that He has abandoned you. When you open the door to those kinds of thoughts, you will find Satan has sown his seeds of deception in your heart.

Satan Dramatizes God's Restrictions

Adam and Eve not only discounted God's goodness, but they also dramatized God's restrictions by adding to them. Nowhere do we find that God told the first humans not to "touch" the forbidden tree. But Eve said to the serpent, "We may eat the fruit of the trees of the garden; but of the fruit of the tree which is in the midst of the garden, God has said, 'You shall not eat it, nor shall you touch it, lest you die'" (Genesis 3:2–3).

But God never said that; He made no mention of "touching." You may say, "Isn't that kind of nitpicking? That isn't that important." But the reality is that when you give Satan an inroad into your life, you will soon be thinking less of the grace of God and more of the law of God.

Satan would love to get you focused on what you can't do rather than what you've been enabled to do. You'll start to think that God isn't interested in your welfare at all, so what difference does it make? Just do whatever you want to do.

That is how deception gets into our lives. That demonic process plays out in young and old alike. It happens to new Christians, as well as to individuals who have been saved for years. It doesn't discriminate against the rich or against the poor. Whoever you are, if you overemphasize the boundaries in your life, you can allow yourself to be deceived.

Satan Diminishes God's Penalty

Finally, Adam and Eve diminished God's penalty for disobedience. In Genesis 2:17, God said that the penalty would be "you shall surely die." But in Genesis 3:3, Eve said the penalty was "lest you die."

Eve left out the "surely die" part and changed it to a simple "lest you die." The latter sounds like death is something that might happen, that it's a possibility. The former makes it clear that death is inevitably connected with sin, that the wages of sin is death. Eve twisted God's words to make them more palatable for disobedience.

In the same manner, it is easy for modern Christians to start reading the Word of God and see "maybe" when the text says "definitely" or to hear "consider" when Scripture says "obey." When you do that, you leave yourself wide open to the deception of Satan.

Just remember that Satan doesn't want to help you; he wants to destroy you. He doesn't want to build you up; he wants to tear you down. He doesn't want to set you free; he wants to enslave you.

The Solution to Deception in the World of the End

What is the solution to our world being driven deeper and deeper into deception? What is the answer to Satan's strategy of deceit? The answer is simple: You deal with deceit by proclaiming the truth. As Jesus said in John 14:6, "I am the way, the truth, and the life."

Jesus doesn't just tell the truth; He is the Truth. That means Jesus is utterly dependable and trustworthy. You can take Him at His word.

Here are three practical things we can do in our everyday lives to help lift the value of truth to a world drowning in deception.

Tell the Truth

Many people feel comfortable with little lies. They call them "white lies."

As a culture, we have convinced ourselves that dishonesty is only dangerous if it actively harms another person. But we are fooling ourselves because the Bible says, "Lying lips are an abomination to the Lord" (Proverbs 12:22).

Because of our identity as children of God and ambassadors of the King, even a little deception can cause massive damage to our lives, to our loved ones, and to our testimonies. For that reason alone, let us speak the truth, the whole truth, and nothing but the truth.

Test the Truth

There is an interesting moment in the book of Acts that is helpful when we think about truth and deception—specifically in terms of the danger that false teachers and false prophets present within the Church. Acts 17:11 says that the Bereans "searched the Scriptures daily to find out whether these things were so."

Do we do that? Do we search the Scriptures daily? The Bereans invested their time and their energy into determining what was true by studying the Scriptures daily. First John 4:1 says, "Beloved, do not believe every spirit, but test the spirits, whether they are of God; because many false prophets have gone out into the world." Don't just tell the truth, test the truth!

Teach the Truth

We can lift up truth in a world of deception by teaching the truth to those who need to hear it. The Bible tells us in the book of Colossians that as believers we are to teach one another.

To the vast majority of modern people, there is no such thing as objective truth. You have your truth, I have my truth, and your truth is no truer than mine. Satan has effectively inserted this false definition of truth into our culture, into our schools, and even into some of our churches. But you cannot be a genuine Christ follower if you embrace this idea.

Every Christian should know and love the truth. Scripture says one of the key characteristics of those who perish and do not go to heaven is that "they did not receive the love of the truth, that they might be saved" (2 Thessalonians 2:10). The clear implication here is that a genuine love for the truth is built into saving faith. It is, therefore, one of the distinguishing qualities of every true believer.

Jesus put it like this: "And you shall know the truth, and the truth shall make you free" (John 8:32). With this thought in our hearts, let's go into this world of deception, lies, and falsehood, and by the grace of God, let's be honest.

APPLICATION

Personal Questions

1. Why do you think the Bible discusses deception in such detail? When did deceit begin (see Genesis 3)?

2. Why do you think deception is so common in our world today?

3. Read Matthew 24:3–4.

   a. Why would Jesus warn us to "take heed that no one deceives [us]" (verse 4)?

   b. Whom, specifically, is Jesus warning us about?

4. What role will deception play in the World of the End?

5. Read Matthew 24:44; 25:13; and Mark 13:32.

   a. Why will imposters claim to be the Messiah or a prophet at this time?

   b. According to these verses, how can we be sure that these are actually imposters?

6. Based on this lesson, how will Satan use his strategy of deception in the World of the End? List and explain the six aspects of his strategy.

7. What is the only way to respond to Satan's deceitfulness? How can you proclaim the truth of Jesus—that He is the Truth—today?

Group Questions

1. As a group, discuss the fall of man in the Garden of Eden (see Genesis 3).

   a. Why was this the moment that deceit entered the world?

   b. Disguised as a serpent, who tempted Eve?

   c. Why do you think Satan is still able to deceive us in our world today?

2. Jesus tells us in Matthew 24:11: "Many false prophets will rise up and deceive many."

   a. What will be the status of deception in the World of the End?

   b. Why will these false prophets reveal themselves at this time?

3. Turn to the section of the lesson titled "The Strategy of Deception in the World of the End" and review it together. Then go back and reread Genesis 3.

   a. Discuss the deceitful ways in which Satan tricked Eve in the garden.

   b. What strategies did Satan use?

4. What is the solution to deception in our world?

5. Read John 14:6. If Jesus speaks the truth, and is Truth Himself, why do you think many people still distrust God's Word?

6. Share how you can tell, test, and teach the truth of Jesus Christ with those around you today.

DID YOU KNOW?

One of the most famous stories of a false messiah came only fifty years after the fall of Jerusalem. In light of that political situation, the Jewish people were ready to follow anyone who would lead them against Rome. A heroic fighter named Simon bar Kokhba appeared and claimed to be the Messiah. He led a revolt known as the Second Jewish Rebellion that resulted in the death of over half a million Jewish people.[1] All that carnage and death resulted from just one man falsely claiming to be the long-awaited Messiah. Jesus' warning was certainly accurate.

Note

1. Sara Toth Stub, "Remembering Hadrian, Destroyer of the Jews," *The Tower*, March 2016, http:// www.thetower.org/article/remembering-hadrian-destroyer-of-the-jews/.

IN A WORLD OF WAR, BE CALM

MATTHEW 24:6–7

In this lesson we learn how to find peace in a world that will always be affected by war.

If you ask someone on the street to define the word *peace*, you might garner responses such as "calm," "quiet," or "tranquil." But one of the dictionary definitions of peace is quite different: "a state or period in which there is no war or a war has ended." It seems that everything in the world is marked by war, even the word *peace*! War will always be with us in this fallen world, but it doesn't need to define us, for Jesus has given a way to exude enduring peace in our lives.

OUTLINE

I. Our Conflicts
   A. The Curse of War
   B. The Cause of War
   C. The Course of War

II. Our Confidence
  A. Peace from God's Promise
  B. Peace from God's Presence
  C. Peace from God's Plan

OVERVIEW

While Egypt is best known for the Great Pyramid of Giza, far to the south near Luxor lies another marvel of the ancient world—the Karnak temple complex. Here you can view some of the oldest remaining ruins in all of history: decayed temples, chapels, and residences from the height of Egypt's power.

Etched onto the wall of one of these temples are hieroglyphics providing a description of the first recorded war in the history of the world. This war wasn't the first conflict in the history of the world, but it was the first recorded conflict in the history of the world. This was the first war written down in enduring form.

The battle described in these hieroglyphics took place on April 16, 1457 BC, between Pharaoh Thutmose III and a coalition of Canaanite tribes. Both armies boasted about ten thousand men. The Canaanites retreated into a walled city known as Megiddo. The Egyptians laid siege to the city and eventually took it in seven months.[1]

All of that is interesting from a historical perspective, but not nearly as interesting as the location of this war. Where exactly did this battle happen?

The battle between Egypt and the Canaanites—the first recorded battle in world history—occurred in the Valley of Armageddon. This conflict is commonly called "The Battle of Megiddo," and the ruins of Megiddo lie today in the country of Israel. From the top of Tel Megiddo, you can view the Valley of Jezreel, also known as the Valley of Armageddon. It's the breadbasket of Israel—a perfect agricultural plain that yields huge amounts of barley, wheat, oranges, and other crops.

But throughout history, the Valley of Megiddo has been the scene of countless battles. It will be at this very spot that the Antichrist will set up his forward operating base in the final war of history—which we know as the Battle of Armageddon.

Our planet has a land surface of more than 57 million square miles, and yet the first and last recorded battles in history will be fought in the very same place. These two wars are like bookends in a history of warfare. Between them lies volume after volume of bloody battles and conflicts that mar the human story.

Our Conflicts

In the Olivet Discourse, Jesus warned that dissention would increase, and consequentially, global warfare would envelope the world in mounting measure. In Matthew 24:6-7, Jesus said, "And you will hear of wars and rumors of wars. See that you are not troubled; for all these things must come to pass, but the end is not yet. For nation will rise against nation, and kingdom against kingdom."

The Curse of War

According to an article in *The New York Times*, the world has been at peace for only 268 out of the past 3,400 years. In other words, only eight percent of our history has been peaceful! And no one really knows how many people have died in times of war. The article speculated that at least 108 million people were killed in wars in the twentieth century alone. And some believe that over a billion people have lost their lives during the military conflicts that have pockmarked history like bomb craters.[2]

C. S. Lewis knew firsthand the curse of war. During World War I, he was sent to the front lines in France where he was wounded by an exploding shell.

Lewis carried his experiences on the front lines with him for the rest of his life. When World War II arrived, he wrote these words:

> My memories of the last war haunted my dreams for years. Military service, to be plain, includes the threat of every temporal evil: pain and death which is what we fear from sickness: isolation from those we love which is what we fear from exile: toil under arbitrary masters, injustice and humiliation, which is what we fear from slavery: hunger, thirst, cold and exposure which

is what we fear from poverty. I'm not a pacifist. If it's got to be, it's got to be. But the flesh is weak and selfish and I think death would be much better than to live through another war.[3]

If you have experienced war at any level, you know exactly what C. S. Lewis is talking about. War is an awful thing, a blight, and a curse to the world. But war is not the worst thing. John Stuart Mill wrote:

War is an ugly thing, but not the ugliest of things: the decayed and degraded state of moral and patriotic feeling which thinks nothing worth a war, is worse.... A man who has nothing which he ... cares more about than he does about his personal safety, is a miserable creature, who has no chance of being free, unless he is made and kept so by the exertions of better men than himself.[4]

While war is awful and brings much sadness and pain, if it were not for those who were willing to fight, we would not be free. Therefore, we are grateful today for those who have served and fought the good fight. Nobody wants war, but nobody wants a world that is not worth sacrifice. And freedom doesn't come free—it comes at a great expense.

The Cause of War

Because the curse of war is so great, philosophers have long searched for the reason behind it. What is the cause of war? Why do wars happen?

The problem is in the human heart, and we can trace it back to the moment Adam and Eve disobeyed God. The vertical rupture between man and God created by sin also formed a horizontal rupture between one person and another. From that fallen day in the Garden forward, history and the pages of the Bible have been marked by war.

In fact, the Old Testament is full of war. The word for war occurs more than three hundred times in the Old Testament Scriptures alone! And more than two hundred times in the Old Testament, Jehovah God is called the Lord of hosts or the Lord of armies.

After Moses and the children of Israel escaped the clutches of Pharaoh through the intervention of Jehovah, they sang this song: "The Lord is a man of war; the Lord is His name" (Exodus 15:3). Many of God's great servants were military men: Saul, David, Moses, Gideon. Consider the testimony of King David: "Blessed be the Lord my Rock, who trains my hands for war, and my fingers for battle" (Psalm 144:1).

This is incredibly important to note because oftentimes in the culture in which we live a military person is not honored as in previous generations. But the Bible honors military men. The Bible honors soldiers. It does not honor war, but it honors those who are willing to fight so that good may prevail and peace can occur.

Some claim that although the Old Testament is full of war, when you arrive at the New Testament and the time of Christ, war disappears from the pages of the Bible. But that is not true. If you read the New Testament, you will discover that while war is not as prevalent, there are five Roman centurions whose lives are told in terms of accommodation and appreciation. All of their stories are positive. There is no negative connotation to war found in the New Testament as some would say.

In fact, the apostles used the language of war on many occasions to illustrate the believer's sojourn. They spoke of "your desires for pleasure that war in your members" (James 4:1). They were told that through Christ they could become "conquerors" (Romans 8:37). Timothy was encouraged by Paul to "wage the good warfare" (1 Timothy 1:18). And these are just a few of the uses of war as a picture of how we are to approach and live the Christian life like soldiers, marching on and battling every single day.

The Course of War
Having looked at the curse of war and the cause of war, let's look at its course. It all started with Adam and Eve bringing sin into the world. Next, Cain killing Abel brought the first murder into existence. And things have only progressed since then.

Throughout history, the technology to kill, maim, and destroy has increased to the point that there is enough military firepower available now to kill everyone on earth many times over. That brings us to the words of Jesus again in Matthew 24:6, "And you will hear of wars and rumors of wars."

As the time comes for Jesus to return, there will be an escalation of verbiage about war. That isn't my opinion; that is Jesus' statement. Remarkably, He spoke those words during a time of relative peace.

There have been only a few years in world history without national and international conflict. Some of those years occurred during the lifetime of Jesus. So when Jesus spoke those words about the coming of war, He was living in a time of relative peace.

Few people would have dared to predict the return and acceleration of international warfare at a time like that. You usually don't talk about war when things are peaceful! But Jesus did because He knew what was ahead. He told His disciples they would hear stories of actual wars and reports of other pending wars.

Some of the Biblical scholars who have commented on the phrase, "wars and rumors of wars," have said that the earliest use of that phrase was a description of world war. In other words, when the writers wrote of wars and rumors of wars, they were talking about world war. If that's the meaning of the phrase, then Jesus was telling His disciples—and us—that before He returned the second time, there would be a world war.

Are we headed toward World War III? Some military experts think so. It is certainly possible that Jesus said so. In either case, the idea is that there will be wars everywhere that will increase in intensity and scope as we draw close to the time when Jesus comes back.

Our Confidence

Now we are all fully aware of the conflicts that besiege us. And there isn't a single thing that you and I can do to stop war. But we can still have confidence and hope today. We can still become the people of God that He created us to be, so that no matter what happens, we will all be ready to stand up and be God's people.

Jesus summarized the source of our confidence in Matthew 24:6: "And you will hear of wars and rumors of wars. See that you are not troubled." After giving us a pretty dire report, Jesus concludes by saying, "Don't worry about it!" That's not the obvious response to news of an impending world war, but that is what Jesus said.

The Greek word for "troubled" in verse 6 means "to be terrified," "to cry aloud," and "to scream." Jesus is telling us not to panic. How can we live in a world like we live in today and not be troubled? Here's the answer: It's all wrapped up in the peace that you find in God's promise, in God's presence, and in God's plan.

Peace from God's Promise

The conflicts that harm and destroy so many innocent people are just grievous. We may ask good questions about why bad things happen. But here is God's promise to us found in Psalm 46:9: "He makes wars cease to the end of the earth." One day King Jesus is going to stop war, and it will never happen again.

Isaiah also spoke of the days when the Kingdom of Jesus will reign from Jerusalem. All the tribes of the earth will hear His teachings and learn His ways. "They shall beat their swords into plowshares, and their spears into pruning hooks; nation shall not lift up sword against nation, neither shall they learn war anymore" (Isaiah 2:4).

One day all war will all be over. If you are a Christian, that should bring hope to your heart. You will not have to live with war for eternity. The King of peace will be in charge, and He will set up His Kingdom on this earth. That should give us great confidence to deal with any combative situation.

Peace from God's Presence

Nothing is more important or more confidence boosting than the promise that God will be with us. There isn't anything we will ever face as followers of Jesus Christ that we will have to face alone. Deuteronomy 20:3–4 puts it this way: "Do not let your heart faint, do not be afraid, and do not tremble or be terrified because of them; for the Lord your God is He who goes with you, to fight for you against your enemies, to save you."

God told Joshua in Joshua 1:9, "Be strong and of good courage; do not be afraid, nor be dismayed, for the Lord your God is with you wherever you go." And in Isaiah 43:2 we are told, "When you pass through the waters, I will be with you."

In fact, the promise of God's presence in our lives is so important that when He sent His Son into the world to provide for our salvation, one of the names He gave Him was Immanuel. "'Behold, the virgin shall be with child, and bear a Son, and they shall call His name Immanuel,' which is translated 'God with us'" (Matthew 1:23).

God is with us. Every day I get up and get ready to face the day, and I know that I am not by myself, for God is with me. And He is with you as well.

When you don't know what is going to happen, when the skies look dark and you're a little bit frightened, just remember God's promise: "I will be with you. I will not leave you nor forsake you" (Joshua 1:5).

Peace from God's Plan

Look again at Matthew 24:6: "And you will hear of wars and rumors of wars. See that you are not troubled; for all these things must come to pass." Notice that Jesus says "must." That single word indicates the indisputable, inexorable decree of Almighty God in all things large and small. Because Jesus knows the things that are going to be fulfilled, we can rest in Him, we can trust in Him, and we can know that His peace is ours no matter what is going on in the world.

That is why Jesus told us that even though we will hear of wars and rumors of wars, we should not be troubled. The only way to do that is to trust. Whom are you trusting in? The One who controls everything! He is the Sovereign God. He is the Almighty. Isaiah put it this way: "You will keep him in perfect peace, whose mind is stayed on You, because he trusts in You" (Isaiah 26:3).

When things are swirling around so unconventionally and uncomfortably, the Bible tells us to concentrate on Jesus. Let your mind be filled with who He is—with His power, His strength, and His sovereignty. Keep your mind stayed upon the Lord.

God is not telling us that war will not happen. He is not telling us that there won't be devastation and sorrow and destruction in the world. What He is saying is this: In Christ you are sufficient. In Christ you are strengthened. In Christ you can be everything you need to be—no matter what is going on in the world.

That is precisely what Jesus says in Matthew 24. Bad times are coming, but Jesus is going to return. But what are we to do until then? Carry on. Be the people God calls us to be. Stand up for righteousness and tell the people we love about Jesus Christ and the glorious hope of salvation only found through Him.

We are not to sit around wringing our hands over what is going to happen. As bad as war can be, as frightening as it might be, it cannot compare to the strength and the peace that God will put in your heart when you put your trust in Him. That is what we need to do.

We live in a world that is warring from Armageddon to Armageddon. But we also serve a mighty and sovereign God who reigns from everlasting to everlasting. So let not your heart be troubled. Be calm. Why? Because Jesus Christ is your Savior. Hallelujah!

APPLICATION

Personal Questions

1. How do you define the word *peace*? Based on this lesson, how can you exude peace in your life?

   times where I have not been in "war"

2. Read Matthew 24:6.

   a. What will we hear rumors of?

   wars and rumors of wars

   b. What should our attitude be when we hear these rumors?

   do not be troubled.

3.   Why do wars take place? Who causes them and why?

4.   What in biblical history is the cause of sin, and ultimately, war?

5.   Why do you think war is predominately written about in the Old Testament?

6.   Does the New Testament still speak of war? If so, is it in a positive or negative light?

7. Read Romans 8:37 and 1 Timothy 1:18. Why does the apostle Paul use war illustrations to demonstrate how we are to live out our Christian life?

8. In light of all the conflicts in the world, how can you still have confidence and hope in Jesus? How would you explain your reasoning to a nonbeliever?

9. In the space below, take a moment to give thanks to God for all the peace that He gives you during the storms of life.

Group Questions

1. As a group, discuss what peace means to you. How do you personally receive it?

2. Read Romans 8:37 and 1 Timothy 1:18 together.

   a. What illustrations of war are mentioned in these verses?

   b. How do these verses depict how we are to approach our Christian walk?

   c. How do these verses strengthen you as you live for Christ?

3. What is the leading cause of war throughout history?

4. Together, compare and contrast the Old Testament with the New Testament. How do each of the testaments depict war? Which one largely explores war throughout its books?

5. During times of war, why should we have confidence? Who is the Source of our peace and a constant presence?

6. Read Psalm 46:9. Discuss as a group how this verse relates to Matthew 24:6.

DID YOU KNOW?

The Jezreel Valley has an incomparable history of warfare. It is where King Saul and the Israelites were defeated (see 1 Samuel 29). It is where King Jehu, who was the son of Jehoshaphat, once and for all eliminated the house of Ahab (see 2 Kings 9). In later history the Greeks, the Romans, and even the Crusaders fought on this plain. In more modern times, Napoleon Bonaparte fought the Ottomans here, calling it the most natural battleground on earth. And the Ottoman army also fought the British there as recently as 1918 in a World War I battle aptly known as "The Battle of Megiddo."

Notes

1. "Battle of Megiddo," *Google Arts & Culture*, accessed July 16, 2022, https://artsandculture.google.com/entity/battle-of-megiddo/m02z596?hl=en.
2. Chris Hedges, "What Every Person Should Know About War," *The New York Times*, July 6, 2003, https://www.nytimes.com/2003/07/06/books/chapters/what-every-person-should-know-about-war.html.
3. C. S. Lewis, *The Joyful Christian* (New York, NY: Touchstone, 1996), 214.
4. John Stuart Mill, "The Contest in America," *Fraser's Magazine*, February 1862.

IN A WORLD OF DISASTERS, BE CONFIDENT

MATTHEW 24:7

In this lesson we see that even during worldwide catastrophes, God is firmly in control.

The cell phone that easily sits in your pocket or purse today has more computing power than the original NASA rockets did in the 1960s. With that kind of advancement within just a generation, you would think the problems of the planet were firmly under control. But nothing could be further from the truth. The COVID-19 pandemic shut down the world. Food shortages and massive inflation are realities. And we have no power to stop all too frequent natural disasters. But over two thousand years ago Jesus predicted this would be our reality.

OUTLINE

I. Global Disasters Are Unavoidable
A. Famines

    B. Plagues

    C. Earthquakes

II. God's Decrees Are Unconditional
    A. Confident in God's Protection
    B. Confident in God's Pardon
    C. Confident in God's Perspective
    D. Confident in God's Provision

OVERVIEW

Many people, including Elon Musk and Jeff Bezos, aspire to someday visit Mars. Most of us won't ever make it that far, but if you ever want to know what if feels like to be on a foreign planet, just take a vacation to Yellowstone National Park!

The terrain at Yellowstone is otherworldly, and at times you feel like you're on the set of a science fiction movie. Part of the that Mars-like feeling can be attributed to the fact that Yellowstone sits on top of an active supervolcano. This is the cause of more than 2,700 earthquakes felt in that area in the year 2021 alone.[1]

Reporter Brad Plumer explains, "Lurking beneath Yellowstone National Park is a reservoir of hot magma five miles deep, fed by a gigantic plume of molten rock welling up from hundreds of miles below." What would happen if that volcano blew? Plumer writes that a major eruption would spew ash for thousands of miles.[2]

Natural disasters are a dynamic part of our world today. But the Bible says they will also be a part of the Last Days and the Tribulation before the Second Coming of Christ. However, these natural disasters are not waiting until the end of history to begin—they are evident today.

According to Jesus' message on the Mount of Olives, earthquakes, famines, plagues, and disasters will continue to increase in intensity and frequency as we draw closer to the day of His return. As He says in Matthew 24:7, "And there will be famines, pestilences, and earthquakes in various places." Let's examine what that means not only for the future, but also for us right now.

Global Disasters Are Unavoidable

There is nothing anyone can do to stop natural disasters from occurring. They are unavoidable, and there is no spot on the planet that is free from their reach. With that being said, the distinction with Jesus' teaching is that as we get closer to the World of the End, natural disasters will become more frequent and intense, just like the birthing pains of a woman in labor. Let's investigate each one of the natural disasters that Jesus said will be a sign of His coming.

Famines

Standing on the Mount of Olives, Jesus used a frightening word, a word which to His disciples recalled a host of Old Testament stories. He said, "There will be famines" (Matthew 24:7). When those four men (Peter, James, John, and Andrew) heard Jesus speak that word, they probably recalled the famine that sent the Israelites to Egypt at the end of Genesis. Or perhaps the famine that drove Naomi and her family to Moab in the book of Ruth. The examples in the history of God's people are plentiful.

In an online report called "Armed Conflict and the Challenge of Hunger," the Global Hunger Index reported that "war and famine, two fearsome horsemen, have long ridden side by side." This sounds like language right out of the book of Revelation! The report also made the following observation:

> Hunger is somehow different from other human stresses. Food and famine strike a deep emotive chord, even among people who have never personally faced starvation. Around the world, people believe that a government that cannot feed its people has forfeited its legitimacy.[3]

Everywhere you look around the world today, there are places where people can't eat because there isn't enough food. And if you look closely, the governments that rule those countries are corrupt and always on the brink of revolution. But this should come as no surprise to those of us who study God's Word because Jesus foresaw the days we're living in.

Plagues

Jesus continued by saying, "And there will be . . . pestilences" (verse 7). The translation of "pestilences" comes from the Greek word *loimos*. This is a term that describes maladies of seasonal sicknesses. The pestilences that Jesus predicted are huge in scale and impact, and they will sweep over large regions of the world and prove difficult to control.

If you go through the Scripture, you will find a strong connection between famine and pestilence in numerous stories. For instance, Moses described the curses that would befall the nation of Israel if they rejected God: "They shall be wasted with hunger, devoured by pestilence" (Deuteronomy 32:24).

Later on, as King Jehoshaphat of Judah was threatened by enemies, he declared his faith in God by saying, "If disaster comes upon us—sword, judgment, pestilence, or famine—we will stand before this temple and in Your presence (for Your name is in this temple), and cry out to You in our affliction, and You will hear and save" (2 Chronicles 20:9).

Thus, what Jesus predicted with famine and plagues is not a random connection. War results in food shortages. And wherever food is scarce, people become nutritionally deprived. Public health then suffers, which creates an ideal environment for disease to flourish.

The twentieth century has had its share of these issues. The Spanish flu pandemic, which came out of World War I, killed more than 40 million people around the world. In the 1950s and 1960s the Asian flu and the Hong Kong flu each resulted in more than a million deaths. The HIV/AIDS epidemic brought an additional 35 million deaths to the world. And in the twenty-first century, we have already seen Swine flu, SARS, MERS, Ebola, and of course, COVID-19.[4]

One would think that advancing medical progress would eradicate disease as wisdom increased through the span of history. But Jesus knew differently. In a world of increasing medical miracles, disease has not been eliminated or eradicated. Instead, sickness is more prevalent than ever. And the trendlines are not encouraging.

Earthquakes

Earthquakes are a part of the future, and if you live along a fault line, you know very well that they are also a part of the present. But there are some interesting things about earthquakes that we should review while looking at the Olivet Discourse.

When God created the world, He designed it with a molten core of boiling magma, covered by a mantle nearly two thousand miles deep. On top of that, surface lands and seas rest on tectonic plates. But sometimes, those plates shift, and the result is an earthquake.

According to Revelation 16:18, when the angel pours out the final bowl of wrath on this world, there will be "a great earthquake, such a mighty and great earthquake as had not occurred since men were on the earth." The ultimate end of the world as we know it today will be from a magnificent earthquake. Isaiah 2:19 describes that moment like this: "They shall go into the holes of the rocks, and into the caves of the earth, from the terror of the Lord and the glory of His majesty, when He arises to shake the earth mightily."

In special times throughout history, there have been earthquakes that have signified that something important was happening. When Moses received the Ten Commandments on Mount Sinai, "the whole mountain quaked greatly" (Exodus 19:18). When Jesus died on Calvary, the ground of Jerusalem quaked (see Matthew 27:51). As you can see, earthquakes are associated with God's power and His judgment.

Much of the natural world is flexible and transitory. Winds and waves come and go, but physical earth is not like that. What is more grounded than the ground? That is why earthquakes are a specific sign of the Creator's control over creation. And this formidable and potent sign will increase in power and frequency as we move toward the end of history.

God's Decrees Are Unconditional

If we're not careful, all this knowledge about the global disasters on the near horizon can make us shake with fear. But the way to combat the fear of these coming events is by supernatural discipleship. The Holy Spirit can give us encouragement, confidence, and hope to face the future.

Confident in God's Protection

We should be reminded of the confidence God gives us in His protection. From Genesis to Revelation, God is revealed as He who watches over His people, keeping them safe in the midst of danger. Throughout the Bible, God is described as the following: our Shield, our Fortress, our Hiding Place, our Keeper, our Refuge, our Rock, our Shade, our Shelter, and our Stronghold. Those are comforting words if you're looking for hope in the midst of uncertainty!

Confident in God's Pardon

Here is an interesting tangent to the Olivet Discourse. Consider these words from Joel 2:12–14: "'Now, therefore,' says the Lord, 'Turn to Me with all your heart, with fasting, with weeping, and with mourning.' So rend your heart, and not your garments; return to the Lord your God, for He is gracious and merciful, slow to anger, and of great kindness; and He relents from doing harm. Who knows if He will turn and relent, and leave a blessing behind Him—a grain offering and a drink offering for the Lord your God?"

It is often through cataclysmic events that God works in the lives of people in different ways, drawing them to the Lord and bringing them to salvation through those turbulent times. When things happen like floods, earthquakes, and famines, they can be blessings because these circumstances can turn our hearts toward God.

Natural disasters bring out supernatural discipleship. And God allows His people to serve those who are hurting and to speak to those needing Christ during these times. In this way, God turns curses into blessings. So don't underestimate how the Lord can use you when difficulty descends on your community or on someone you know.

Confident in God's Perspective

Don't be confident only in God's protection and in His pardon, be confident in His perspective as well. We can place our full confidence in God because He tells us exactly how it's all going to end. We're on a journey, and there's a destination. We are going toward something. "And I heard a loud voice from heaven saying, 'Behold, the tabernacle of God is with men, and He will dwell with them, and they shall be His people. God

Himself will be with them and be their God. And God will wipe away every tear from their eyes; there shall be no more death, nor sorrow, nor crying. There shall be no more pain, for the former things have passed away'" (Revelation 21:3–4).

One of the best ways we can communicate hope during times of disaster is to tell everyone that what we are going through is temporary. This world is not our home.

The Bible tells us that we have a lot to look forward to—let's not forget that! Yes, there will be some difficult days. Natural disasters reflect the fallen nature of our world. But these calamities that we experience are only temporary. And each disaster reminds us that a disaster-free eternity is awaiting us. Each of these difficult events should inspire our hearts to long for our eternal home.

Confident in God's Provision

Finally, we can find comfort in a gem found in the Lord's Prayer. In Matthew 6:11, Jesus prays, "Give us this day our daily bread." God will provide for our needs on a daily basis.

Remember the Old Testament story about the widow of Zarephath? She used her last bit of flour and oil to make bread for Elijah, but from that moment on, there was always flour in her bin and oil in her jar. God just kept providing for her. It was an absolute miracle.

During the war between Russia and Ukraine in 2022, Daniil Kiriluk lived in one of the hardest hit areas of Ukraine. He and his wife have ten sons and nine daughters, and he is the pastor of a small church made up of his large family and about twenty others. Amid their own struggles, this large family decided to make bread and share it with those affected by the war. In one night, they baked thirty loaves of bread.

As people came to get the bread, others brought flour. And the more bread they made, the more flour they had. All the Kiriluk children and grandchildren helped, bringing the total number of workers in the home to 33. Soon the church was producing 160 loaves per day, and more than one ton of flour was donated to their efforts.

But it wasn't only bread that was distributed. Gospel newspapers went out with every loaf. One couple in the church with a distinct gift of evangelism shared the message of Jesus as the Bread of Life. If you were to see the picture of this family lined up by size, you'd praise God for such people whose hope overflows with kindness and evangelism in times of great danger—aided by God's provision.[5]

The Bible says that God will provide, and there is no doubt that He will and that He always does. But God does some of His best work through people. And not special people like Moses and Paul, but simple people just like you and me.

One of the best things we can do when we're feeling a little bit anxious about what is going on in the world is to stop thinking about ourselves and look around and start thinking about whom we can help. Can you imagine the joy that comes to your heart when you're able to help somebody who's really in need? Suddenly your fear completely disappears.

This is not a time for those of us who are followers of Jesus to cling to our possessions. When things get bad, people tend to think they can't give money to the church or missions or be generous with what they have. But that is the worst thing we can do. Instead, we need to manage the resources God gives us to help other people.

If you're a Christian, you simply need to ask the Lord to show you a need that you can respond to. Maybe you can make bread like the Kiriluk family. Maybe you can volunteer to repair someone's car that has broken down. I don't know how God uses you or how He uses me, but I know that the Bible teaches us that the perilous times of life are the times for you and me as believers to stand up strong and be the people of God we were called to be.

Let's make a difference in our culture. Let's make it better by helping others. If we do that, God will use us in ways that we can't even comprehend. We are living in a time of great opportunity to serve Him because the need is so great.

And here is even better news: Our Father is in our ear, and He tells us what to do. So if He tells you to turn right, turn right! If He tells you to give somebody something, give it to them. Listen to your Father because He is the only One who knows what the future holds. There is no way for you and me to guess what is coming, so we should joyfully trust and obey in the tasks that He has set before us.

If you really believe that God is in your heart and that He is in your ear, you won't go to bed at night with anxiety and fear about the future. Instead, you will rest easy knowing that the Creator of all the universe is still in charge of the future. You will be able to wake up in the morning with peace, knowing that whatever may lie ahead, God is with you. You can be confident in the midst of the storm.

APPLICATION

Personal Questions

1. What will continue to increase in intensity and frequency until the Lord returns?

2. Read Matthew 24:7. Do you think "famines, pestilences, and earthquakes" will take place right now, in the future, or both?

3. Write down a current natural disaster. Do you think it is part of the "beginning of birth pains" (Matthew 24:8 NIV) that Jesus spoke of? Why or why not?

4. Why are global disasters unavoidable? Why do you think Jesus told us that they will only increase as His return draws nearer?

5. Famines were common throughout stories written in the Old Testament. Why do you think famine and war go hand in hand?

6. What is the commonality between famine and pestilence in the Scriptures?

7. Read Revelation 16:18. What great event is set to occur from an earthquake?

   a. Read Exodus 19:18 NIV and Matthew 27:51. What great events have already occurred from earthquakes?

   b. Because of these verses, what can we associate earthquakes with?

8. Based on this lesson, we know that God's decrees are unconditional. With that in mind, fill in the blanks below. We should be confident in . . .

   a. God's _____.

   b. God's _____.

   c. God's _____.

   d. God's _____.

Group Questions

1. Why do you think global disasters will only continue to get worse as we wait on the Lord to return? Discuss as a group.

2. Why would Jesus describe these disasters as "birth pains" in Matthew 24:8 NIV?

3. Together, name some current global disasters. Next, share whether or not you think they are part of the "birth pains" Jesus described.

4. Jesus said, "There will be famines," in Matthew 24:7. What biblical events about famines do you think the apostles recalled from the Old Testament (see Genesis 42 and Ruth 1)?

5. Compare and contrast famine with pestilence. In what way do they relate to war?

6. Read 2 Chronicles 20:9. Why would King Jehoshaphat say, "If disaster comes upon us . . . sword, judgment, pestilence, or famine"?

   a. Based on this verse, do you think Jesus' prophecy is a coincidence?

   b. Why or why not?

7. Traditionally, earthquakes symbolize what?

8. What are the four points of God's unconditional decrees that should give us confidence and hope about the future? Review them together.

9. How can the Lord's Prayer give you comfort for the future?

10. In the space below, write down a prayer of gratitude for God's continued protection in your life.

DID YOU KNOW?

One of the great famines described in the Bible happened during the reign of evil King Ahab and his equally wicked wife, Jezebel. God told Elijah to announce to Ahab that there would be a great famine and that it would only be broken by Elijah's command. God withheld all rain from Israel for an astounding three and a half years, which created a severe famine (see 1 Kings 18:2). Only after Elijah patiently prayed seven times on the top of Mount Carmel did God send a small cloud from over the sea to Samaria, which soon engulfed the area with torrential rain.

Notes

1. Michael Poland, "2,773 Earthquakes Were Recorded in the Yellowstone National Park Area in 2021, Annual Report Says," *Idaho Capital Sun*, May 3, 2022, https://idahocapitalsun.com/2022/05/03/2773-earthquakes-were-recorded-in-the-yellowstone-national-park-area-in-2021-annual-report-says/.
2. Brad Plumer, "What Would Happen If the Yellowstone Supervolcano Actually Erupted?" *Vox*, December 15, 2014, https://www.vox.com/2014/9/5/6108169/yellowstone-supervolcano-eruption.
3. "Armed Conflict and the Challenge of Hunger: Is an End in Sight?" *Global Hunger Index*, October 2015, https://www.globalhungerindex.org/issues-in-focus/2015.html.
4. Nicholas LePan, "Visualizing the History of Pandemics," *Visual Capitalist*, March 14, 2020, https://www.visualcapitalist.com/history-of-pandemics-deadliest/.
5. Pastor Foley, "Ukraine: Church Leader and His 19 Children Bake One Ton of Bread, Share Gospel in War Zone," *Do the Word*, April 5, 2022, https://dotheword.org/2022/04/05/ukraine-church-leader-and-his-19-children-bake-one-ton-of-bread-share-gospel-in-war-zone/.

IN A WORLD OF PERSECUTION, BE PREPARED

MATTHEW 24:9

In this lesson we learn that there will be a day when all Christians will pay a price for their faith.

When we think of Christian persecution, the first image that usually comes to mind is of a missionary couple in a foreign country paying the price for their faith. And while that is not entirely inaccurate, the reality is that attacks on Christian values and even the Christian faith in general are skyrocketing in modern Western societies. The time is soon coming when there won't be anywhere to escape punishment for expressing faith in Jesus Christ.

OUTLINE

I. **The Record of Christian Persecution**

II. **The Reality of Christian Persecution**
   A. Tribulation

B. Martyrdom

C. Hatred

III. The Response to Christian Persecution

A. Recount Your Blessing

B. Respond with Worship

C. Reevaluate Your Suffering

D. Receive Your Reward

OVERVIEW

Andrew and Norine Brunson were relaxing at a Turkish retreat on the Aegean Sea when the phone rang. "Andrew," said the voice, "the police have just been here looking for you." The call was from the small church that Andrew had pastored for 24 years in the New Testament city of Smyrna, located in Turkey.

That was the beginning of a nightmare that lasted 735 days. As he later recounted in his memoir, he was held in a small prison cell with nothing but a low bunk, meaning he had to be either standing, walking, or laying on the bed at all times. The toilet didn't flush. And worst of all, his Bible and glasses were taken away.

Pastor Brunson was sometimes housed in overcrowded cells and was unable to sleep because of the stifling heat. A third of the way into the ordeal, he sobbed to the prison doctor, "I can't handle it. I have constant panic, I don't sleep. I have lost fifty pounds. I have fought for eight months to control myself, and I can't handle it anymore." More than once, he said he was afraid he was going insane.

But the Lord didn't forsake Andrew Brunson. He later said, "Each day I focused on fighting through my fear to reach a place where I surrendered myself to whatever God had ahead for me . . . God was teaching me to stand in the dark, to persevere apart from my feelings, perceptions, and circumstances."[1] He had to learn the lesson of Isaiah 50:10. "Let the one who walks in the dark, who has no light, trust in the name of the Lord and rely on their God" (NIV).

Not long ago, Andrew Brunson spoke again. His words were very sobering as he warned of the persecution ahead for the Western church. Here is what he said:

> I believe the pressures that we're seeing in our country now are going to increase, and one of these pressures is going to be hostility toward people who embrace Jesus Christ and his teaching, who are not ashamed to stand for him. . . . My concern is that we're not ready for this pressure. And not being prepared is very, very dangerous.[2]

Andrew wants us to be prepared. I want us to be prepared. And Jesus wants us to be prepared. One of the best ways to be prepared for this hostility is to heed Jesus' words in Matthew 24:9: "Then you will be handed over to be persecuted and put to death, and you will be hated by all nations because of me" (NIV).

The Record of Christian Persecution

How long has there been persecution for followers of Christ? Ever since Jesus Christ was on this earth! He Himself was rejected, scourged, and crucified. The book of Isaiah even described Jesus as a "Man of sorrows" (53:3).

The early disciples of Christ were arrested, whipped, and forbidden to preach in the Name of Jesus. They, though, would not be silenced. As you may recall, Stephen became the first person to die for his faith in Christ. The entire chapter of Acts 7 is devoted to telling the story of his martyrdom.

By now in our modern and sophisticated world, you would think there would be a decrease in the persecution of those pledging personal faith in Christ. Sadly, that is not true.

In many parts of the globe, the persecution of Christians now exceeds any period in history. According to Dr. Todd M. Johnson of Gordon Conwell Seminary, more than seventy million Christians have been martyred throughout history, and more than half of those deaths occurred in the twentieth century! He also estimates that one million

Christians were killed between 2001 and 2010, and another 900,000 between 2011 and 2020.[3]

The Reality of Christian Persecution

Every year, the Christian charity Open Doors releases a "World Watch List" highlighting the fifty places where faith in Jesus costs the most. In 2022, Afghanistan, North Korea, Somalia, Libya, and Yemen topped the list. Furthermore, they estimate that 360 million Christians in the world today experience extreme persecution because of their faith. One out of every seven believers lives under the pressure of persecution![4]

But Jesus saw all this coming. He isn't caught off guard, and He didn't want us to be caught off guard. That is why He said, "Then they will deliver you up to tribulation and kill you, and you will be hated by all nations for My name's sake" (Matthew 24:9). Each phrase in that prophecy is important. Let's analyze them one by one.

Tribulation

Jesus began by saying, "Then they will deliver you up to tribulation." "Tribulation" comes from a Greek word that describes a grinding pressure. The word is best used in the context for the grinding of wheat. Think of how they ground grain in the ancient world. The kernels were pounded and pulverized between two millstones with no chance of relief.

That is tribulation in a nutshell. And that is what Christ has promised we will experience if we follow Him. That begs the question: Are we already feeling that kind of persecution and tribulation? The answer is "Yes." Here are two stories that typify what is going on in the world.

In Kaduna state, Nigeria, a group of Fulani herdsmen attacked 4 villages, killing 18 Christians while burning down 92 houses. The victims were specifically targeted because of their faith in Jesus Christ.[5] And in Eastern Uganda, a man converted to Christianity, even though he was the head of a private Muslim school. When the teachers at the school heard him praying in Jesus' name, they beat him, scarred him with third-degree burns, and fired him from his position.[6]

There are hundreds of stories like that that come across the wires every day. They can discourage you and make you feel sad for the people who are being persecuted. But Jesus said this time would come, and no one is immune from it.

Martyrdom

Notice Jesus' second promise in verse 9: "Then they will... kill you." From persecution to murder. But it is true that the World of the End will see a dramatic increase in martyrdom and religious killings—not only in regions of the world dominated by Islam and Hinduism and socialism, but in all nations.

The Bible uses the word *martyr* to describe someone who is slain for their faith. The first instance of this word is used in Acts 22:20: "And when the blood of Your martyr Stephen was shed." The word *martyr* means "witness." Specifically, it is one who dies because of their witness for Jesus Christ.

Kayla Mueller understood that reality. As a Christian, she believed it was her responsibility to join in God's work of relieving suffering in the world. "I find God in the suffering eyes reflected in mine," she once wrote. Addressing God, she added, "If this is how you are revealed to me this is how I will forever seek you."[7]

While serving as a relief worker in Syria, Kayla was taken hostage by members of an ISIS cell. She remained a prisoner for eighteen months, enduring unimaginable abuse of every kind along with several other female captives. She eventually become a personal prisoner of Abu Bakr al-Baghdadi, the leader of ISIS at the time.

When a group of young women made a plan to escape their captors, she refused to join them. "I am an American. If I escape with you, they will do everything to find us again."[8] The four women did escape, and they even smuggled out a letter that Kayla wanted to give to her parents.

Kayla Mueller died at the hands of her captor, Abu Bakr al-Baghdadi. Yet she is victorious today because her story is proving once again that the power of light is greater than the power of darkness. Love over hate is always the right equation. Kayla's witness will forever reveal the power of the Gospel—a power that endures even in the face of death.

Hatred

Jesus then told Peter, James, John, and Andrew that "you will be hated by all nations for My name's sake." Have you ever experienced anything negative because people know that you are a Christian? Have you ever felt any fear, anguish, or even rejection because people know that you're a Christian? This is all part of the cost of following Christ.

One of the grimmer realities of Jesus' revelation in this verse is that persecution against His followers is not clinical or detached. No, the persecution of God's people during the World of the End will be fueled by emotion and hatred. Such hatred is unwarranted, but for two thousand years the world has raged against us in many forms. They have sought to disband the movement that Jesus began and to ban the Bible that He gave us. They have sought to disrupt the ministries He started and to destroy the souls that He saved.

What motivates people to do that? Christians try to help their neighbors and make the world a better place wherever they are established. The world is motivated to hate us because their hatred goes back to who Jesus is and what He has done. He came to deal with sin. He came not to condemn the world "but that the world through Him might be saved" (John 3:17). Jesus offers salvation!

But in order to be saved, you have to admit that you are lost! Many people don't want to deal with the reality of their sin. They think they're pretty good. They think they have it made. They think they're good enough to go to heaven without God—they don't need Jesus.

Note that Jesus gave us the very reason the nations would hate us: "for My name's sake." The reason Christians experience persecution is because we have aligned ourselves with Jesus Christ, and the world hates Jesus Christ. In John 15:18, Jesus said, "If the world hates you, you know that it hated Me before it hated you." He later added in John 15:20, "If they persecuted Me, they will also persecute you."

It is important to clarify just what persecution is because some use it as a cover word for what is negative in their lives. But persecution is solely what happens to you particularly because you are a Christian, a follower of Jesus Christ. One day we will have to stand up for our faith, and when we do, we will be persecuted. Jesus warned us because He wants us to be ready.

The Response to Christian Persecution

Whenever possible, we need to stand up kindly and bravely for the freedom that allows us our faith. In some places, there is no concept of religious liberty. Followers of Christ will have to navigate the best way to handle instances of persecution.

Above all, we need to honor the Lord with our lives. We should not be cowardly or cover up our faith because it is under attack. We are to be God's people unashamedly in a gracious, godly way, starting with recounting our blessings.

Recount Your Blessings

One of the most enigmatic verses in the Bible is Matthew 5:10, "Blessed are those who are persecuted for righteousness' sake, for theirs is the kingdom of heaven." How could Jesus join "blessed" and "persecuted" in the same sentence, talking about the same people?

The key is to understand that being persecuted by the world is a reminder that we are not of the world. We are members of God's Kingdom, we are children in His family, and the world is not our home. Therefore, we can choose to minimize the importance of what we experience in the world because it does not matter in the face of eternity.

And so, it is a backdoor blessing when people persecute you. It reminds you that you are on the right road and headed in the right direction. You are headed toward heaven.

Respond with Worship

If there was anyone in history who understand the reality of what it is like to be persecuted, it was the apostle Paul. From the moment he accepted Christ, he was forced to deal with haranguers and harassers who wanted him dead. He scaled city walls in a basket. He endured beatings and stonings. He was arrested and accused. He was shipwrecked and snake bitten. All these things occurred because he refused to let go of Christ.

On one particular occasion, Paul and Silas were beaten with rods and tossed into a Macedonian jail. Scripture says the jailer even fastened their feet into stocks, leaving them in a torturous position, not being able to move their legs (see Acts 16:24). How did they respond? "But at midnight Paul and Silas were praying and singing hymns to God, and the prisoners were listening to them" (Acts 16:25).

After being stripped, beaten, locked up, and left to suffer, Paul and Silas were praying and singing hymns to God. They chose to praise God in the middle of horrible circumstances. Praise is a weapon we can choose to respond to persecution with. When the time comes, I pray that you and I will have the courage and resolve to worship even in the midst of mistreatment. If we do, God will get the glory, and the victory will be ours.

Reevaluate Your Suffering

Consider the words of Paul found in Romans 8:18: "For I consider that the sufferings of this present time are not worthy to be compared with the glory which shall be revealed in us." Someday when we are in heaven experiencing the bliss and joy of being in the presence of Almighty God, we will realize that the temporary suffering we endured here on earth pales in comparison with the wonders of God and our eternal home in heaven.

Receive Your Reward

In the book of Revelation, Jesus directed seven letters to seven churches. One of those churches was in the town of Smyrna. This specific church went through great suffering in that city. Here is what Jesus had to say to this church: "Do not fear any of those things which you are about to suffer. Indeed, the devil is about to throw some of you into prison, that you may be tested, and you will have tribulation ten days. Be faithful until death, and I will give you the crown of life" (Revelation 2:10).

I encourage you to remember Jesus' words: "Do not fear any of those things." We have nothing to be afraid of because God is in control. You are on the winning team, and you are going to win. And the reward is nothing short of the crown of life.

The gates of hell and Satan cannot prevail against the Church of Jesus Christ. Whether we live or die, the Gospel is true. And the Gospel is true whether you believe it or not or whether you accept it or not. It has always been true, and it will always be true because the Gospel is Jesus. And Jesus is the Truth!

So in a world of persecution, we must be vigilant, and we must be prepared. But we don't need to be anxious. God will give you grace exactly when you need it. When the time comes to stand up for your faith, you'll know what to do because God will show you what to do. By His Spirit, you will be able to take a stand for Jesus Christ.

And when you do that, the Bible promises that you will feel a sense of God's presence like you have never felt before. You will be blessed and reminded that the Christian life isn't just all about the good things God provides—it is about the testimony we have in this world to which He has called us. We need to stand up and be God's people and not worry about the future because God has it under control.

APPLICATION

Personal Questions

1. In response to the growing amount of persecution toward Christians, what should we be prepared for?

   a. How do you believe Jesus wants you to be prepared?

   b. In what ways can you be prepared?

   c. Who can help you be prepared?

2. Read Matthew 24:9. What are followers of Christ promised? List the promises below.

3. There has always been persecution toward Christ's followers. Why do you think that is?

    a. How were the first followers of Jesus persecuted?

    b. According to 2 Corinthians 11:24–29, what did the apostle Paul endure?

4. Read Acts 7.

    a. Who was the first person to die for their faith in Christ?

    b. What did he say as he was being killed (see verses 59–60)?

5. Jesus said the world would hate Christians for His "name's sake" in Matthew 24:9. Read John 15:18 and then explain why that is.

6. What should be our response to persecution?

    a. According to Matthew 5:10, what should we remember?

    b. Why is persecution a reminder that we are not of this world? To Whom do we belong?

    c. How did Paul and Silas respond to persecution in Acts 16:25?

7. Why should we not "fear any of those things which [we] are about to suffer" (Revelation 2:10)?

Group Questions

1. Discuss what could have contributed to the rise of persecution throughout the twentieth century.

2. Based on this lesson, is persecution inevitable? Why or why not?

3. Are you currently facing some type of pressure or persecution for your faith in Christ? If so, share with the group.

4. Jesus said, "They will deliver you up to tribulation and kill you" (Matthew 24:9). Why are we promised to face tribulation for our faith?

   a. Whom does the world hate (see John 15:18)?

   b. What does the term *martyr* mean to you? Discuss.

   c. Who was the first martyr of the Christian faith (see Acts 7; 22:20)?

5. What emotion fuels the persecution of Christians worldwide?

6. As Christians, how are we to respond to those who persecute us? Explain why this is.

a. In what ways can we recount our blessings (see Matthew 5:10)?

b. How can we respond with worship to God?

c. How did Paul reevaluate his suffering (see Romans 8:18)?

7. Read Revelation 2:10 together.

a. How does this verse give you comfort?

b. What crown is awaiting us in heaven?

c. In the face of persecution, how can you be vigilant in standing up for your faith in Christ Jesus?

DID YOU KNOW?

Eleven of the twelve disciples of Jesus perished violently as martyrs for the Gospel. According to tradition, Thomas was impaled by a spear for preaching the Good News. Bartholomew, the most widely traveled of the disciples after Jesus' death and resurrection, was skinned alive and crucified for his faith. Peter was famously crucified in Rome by Nero in AD 68 but demanded to be crucified upside down as he considered himself unworthy to be crucified like Jesus. Only John, eventually banished to the island of Patmos where he wrote the book of Revelation, was not martyred, living to an old age (see Revelation 1:9).

Notes

1. Andrew Brunson with Craig Borlase, *God's Hostage* (Grand Rapids, MI: Baker Books, 2019), 79, 93, 105.
2. "'Hostility Toward People Who Embrace Jesus Christ': Pastor Brunson Predicts Intensified Persecution of US Christians," *CBN News*, December 10, 2020, https://www1.cbn.com/cbnnews/us/2020/december/hostility-toward-people-who-embrace-jesus-christ-pastor-brunson-predicts-intensified-persecution-of-us-christians.
3. Dr. Todd M. Johnson, "Christian Martyrdom: Who? Why? How?" *Gordon Conwell Theological Seminary*, December 18, 2019, https://www.gordonconwell.edu/blog/christian-martyrdom-who-why-how/.
4. "Discover the 50 Places Where Faith in Jesus Costs the Most," *Open Doors*, accessed May 11, 2022, https://www.opendoorsusa.org/2022-world-watch-list-report/.
5. Morning Star News Nigeria Correspondent, "Herdsmen and Others Kill 18 Christians in Northern Nigeria," *Christian Headlines*, May 2, 2022, https://www.christianheadlines.com/blog/herdsmen-and-others-kill-18-christians-in-northern-nigeria.html.
6. Morning Star News East Africa Correspondent, "Head of Islamic School Burned, Fired for Becoming Christian," *Christian Headlines*, April 18, 2022, https://www.christianheadlines.com/blog/head-of-islamic-school-burned-fired-for-becoming-christian.html.
7. Carl and Marsha Mueller, "Remarks by Carl and Marsha Mueller," *Permanent Observer Mission of the Holy See to the United States*, April 28, 2016, https://holyseemission.org/contents//events/5723cc24e92a84.35067264.php.
8. Jim Denison, "ISIS Martyr Kayla Mueller's Amazing Faith," *Christian Headlines*, August 26, 2016, https://www.christianheadlines.com/columnists/denison-forum/isis-martyr-kayla-mueller-s-amazing-faith.html.

IN A WORLD OF BETRAYAL, BE FAITHFUL

MATTHEW 24:10

In this lesson we learn about the painful reality of betrayal in the world.

There are many occasions in life that cause pain and anguish. The sudden loss of a loved one can be devastating. Financial ruin and economic hardship can lead to many tearful and sleepless nights. But there is a special kind of pain that can only be associated with a violation of trust—when someone you let into your world purposely betrays you. Jesus warned us that this treacherous act will only increase as the day beckons for His return.

OUTLINE

I. **The Pain of Betrayal**

II. **The Portraits of Betrayal**

III. The Prophecy of Betrayal
   A. A World of Offense
   B. A World of Betrayal
   C. A World of Hatred

IV. The Preparation for Betrayal
   A. Choose Your Friends Carefully
   B. Stay Focused on Your Purpose
   C. Pursue Loyalty
   D. Do Good to Those Who Hate You
   E. Count on the Character of God

OVERVIEW

The man strolling through a public park in Fairfax County, Virginia, didn't look like one of the world's most dangerous spies. He was a typical middle-aged, middle-class man who was a bit out of shape. But looks can be deceiving.

That man, Robert Hanssen, was an FBI agent with top security clearance. Unbeknownst to the federal government, he had been betraying his country for almost two decades as a double agent. Starting in 1979, he sold thousands of U.S. classified files to the Russians, including detailed military plans for responding to a nuclear war. He even betrayed fellow American operatives, some of whom were executed by the Russians.[1]

However, the FBI was watching on that day—February 18, 2001—when he made a dead drop delivery beneath the bridge in Foxstone Park. As they swarmed and cuffed him, Hanssen asked one question: "What took you so long?"

Between 1979 and 2001, Hanssen had betrayed his country time and again. The FBI's official statement reveals the depth of his treachery:

> A betrayal of trust by an FBI Agent, who is not only sworn to enforce the law but specifically to help protect our nation's security, is particularly abhorrent. This kind of criminal conduct

represents the most traitorous action imaginable against a country governed by the Rule of Law.[2]

What a bitter phrase: a betrayal of trust. A man like Robert Hanssen occasionally makes the headlines and history books, but acts of betrayal happen every day in politics, business, and life. Perhaps you've been damaged by someone who broke trust with you and in the process broke your heart.

What does this have to do with the World of the End? It turns out that Jesus specifically included betrayal in His list of trends that would intensify before His Second Coming: "And then many will be offended, will betray one another, and will hate one another" (Matthew 24:10). Just like deceit, natural disasters, and war, we will experience betrayal in greater measure as we move together toward the end of history.

The Pain of Betrayal

Few things in life hurt us worse than personal betrayal. Betrayal is one of the strongest words on the emotional scale. We don't use it lightly. What makes betrayal so raw and painful is that it comes not from our enemies, but from those we believed were our friends—or even from our family.

People can't betray us unless we've put down our guard and trusted them. Betrayal exposes and exploits our vulnerability. It wounds more deeply than other deceits because it makes us subject to a double cross. As Les Parrott wrote, "[Backstabbers] put on a front that appears accommodating, loyal, and yes, even sacrificial. Then, without warning, they raise their knife, and by the time you see the glint of the blade, it's almost always too late."[3]

Perhaps you've shared your most private thoughts with someone only to discover they betrayed your confidence and told someone else. Maybe you paid someone in advance for work without getting what you'd bargained for. Far more painful than that is discovering your spouse cheated on you or that a sibling has lied to you.

Every evening, people all over the world go to bed with the feeling that they were burned by someone. Such pain lingers on for a very long time. Many of them seek to forgive and move on, but it's a hard and painful process.

The Portraits of Betrayal

Don't get into the line of thinking that betrayal is a recent development in the sinful life of man; there is nothing new about being betrayed by someone. The sin of betrayal goes back to a cryptic point before the beginning of human history itself when the archangel Lucifer turned against his Creator.

The Lord told Lucifer in Ezekiel 28:14, "I ordained and anointed you as the mighty angelic guardian. You had access to the holy mountain of God" (NLT). But this mighty angel deserted his God and instead, led a host of angels in rebellion against Him. Ever since that point, betrayal has cascaded through the human story like falling dominos.

Adam and Eve were seduced by Satan. Cain betrayed his own brother, Abel. Jacob double-crossed his brother Esau out of his inheritance. Delilah viciously betrayed Samson, costing him his power and his life. And the psalms of David are filled with anguish over various acts of betrayal—including an attempted coup by his own son, Absalom.

There are many more examples found throughout Scripture, but only one matches the horrendous betrayal of Satan against God, and that is the betrayal of Judas Iscariot against Jesus. Luke 22:3–4 tells us, "Then Satan entered Judas, surnamed Iscariot, who was numbered among the twelve. So he went his way and conferred with the chief priests and captains, how he might betray Him to them."

When we study the character of Judas in the Bible, almost every reference includes his act of betrayal. Luke describes him as "Judas Iscariot who also became a traitor" (Luke 6:16). He committed the worst act of treason in history, selling out the Son of God for thirty pieces of silver. For this act alone, even today the word *Judas* is a synonym for traitor.

The Prophecy of Betrayal

In Matthew 24:10, Jesus breaks down betrayal into three layers of severity: "And then many will be offended, will betray one another, and will hate one another." Have you noticed how many of Jesus' prophetic promises in the Olivet Discourse are connected to emotional wounds? Prophecy is about more than earthquakes, pestilence, and heavenly signs. It's also about offenses, betrayal, and hatred. Every word of Jesus is intentional, so let's trace this trio of terms.

A World of Offense

The word "offended" that Jesus uses in verse 10 is a translation of the Greek term *skandalizo*, from which we get our modern words *scandal* or *scandalized*. That term is used thirty times in the New Testament, and it refers to a hidden foot trap in the ground that causes someone to stumble and fall.

At some point in your life, you've surely tripped on a loose piece of concrete or an unseen root popping out of the ground. If you were walking briskly, it probably sent you sprawling. That is the very picture Jesus painted with the term *skandalizo*. The main idea is that Satan uses other people around us to set traps for us. That's what it means to trip others up—to be a stumbling block. As the Lexham English Bible says, "And then many will be led into sin."

A World of Betrayal

The Greek word for "betray" is *paradidomi*. This is a relatively common word found in the New Testament as it used on 121 occasions. This term can be translated into several English words, including *deliver*, *betray*, and *give over*. In the context of Matthew 24, it paints the picture of Christians attempting to escape persecution by delivering over other Christians to be judged, punished, or even killed.

The saddest part of Matthew 24:10 is the repeated phrase "one another." Christians will betray Christians. Or perhaps more accurately, people who claim to be Christians will betray those who really are.

Earlier we referenced some of the more infamous examples of betrayal in the Bible, but there is one to be added to the list—Alexander the coppersmith. Many commentators believe we first meet him in 1 Timothy 1:20, when he was declaring falsehoods about God among the church-goers in Ephesus.[4]

Paul removed Alexander from the fellowship of the church, along with another heretic named Hymenaeus. According to 1 Timothy 1:20, Paul delivered them "to Satan that they may learn not to blaspheme." That should be the end of the story, but sadly, it is not.

Many commentators believe Alexander harbored a deep bitterness toward Paul and eventually betrayed Paul's whereabouts to Roman authorities. This led to Paul's final arrest, perhaps in Troas. All this took place during the most dangerous days the Church had yet experienced, when Emperor Nero declared Christians public enemies of the Roman government.

If this scenario is correct, Alexander's betrayal led to the imprisonment, trial, and execution of the greatest evangelist and missionary in Christian history. In the final chapter known to be written by Paul, he told Timothy, "Alexander the coppersmith did me much harm. May the Lord repay him according to his works. You also must beware of him, for he has greatly resisted our words" (2 Timothy 4:14–15).

Do we see current evidence of Christians being betrayed by family members, neighbors, or even so-called Christian brothers and sisters? Yes. Terrible persecution is afflicting the Church in many countries. And especially intense pressure is often placed on believers to give up the names of other Christians.

That sounds like what may happen during the Tribulation when raw evil will operate on steroids. The machinery of the Antichrist will seek to track down every new believer and force from them the names of other converts. But as we've seen, those birth pains are already occurring.

A World of Hatred

As appalling as betrayal is, hatred is even worse. Someone may be tricked into betraying you, or they may do so out of weakness. But when the motivation is hatred for you, it's reached a new level of evil. Recall that Jesus said in Matthew 24:10, "At that time many will turn away from the faith and will betray and hate each other" (NIV).

This is the second time Jesus has mentioned hate in the Olivet Discourse. In verse 9, He warned that the world would hate us, which is a hatred coming from outside the Church. But in verse 10, he warned that Christians or so-called Christians would "betray one another, and...hate one another"— Jesus was warning of hatred from within the Church.

We need to realize that genuine followers of Christ—those who are abiding in Christ and growing in Him—are not the sources of hate but the objects of it. Institutionalized religion and apostate Christianity, however, will always be vengeful against true believers.

That is why we need to keep all forms of hatred, resentment, and bitterness out of our hearts. I see Christians verbally abuse other Christians over their political beliefs, their financial expenditures, or their worship styles. Church fights always cause collateral damage.

Not all of Christ's followers are equally mature, so seasoned Christians should set the model for those who are still babes in Christ. We shouldn't let divisive topics of secondary importance break the bond of fellowship between members of God's Kingdom.

The Preparation for Betrayal

I don't need to convince you that betrayal is painful, nor persuade you that backstabbing is commonplace in our world. You've seen it, and you've felt it. The real questions are: What can we do about it? How do we respond to the reality of betrayal both now and in the future? How do we prepare for it?

The answer: We must be faithful! Let's examine five simple steps to take right now as we seek to shine the light of God's goodness and grace in a world struggling with disloyalty.

Choose Your Friends Carefully

It is amazing how we are influenced by the friends we choose. It is frightening how easily we're drawn into unhealthy relationships! Our needs can overcome our judgment, and our feelings can overrule common sense. Before we know it, we can find ourselves in a relationship that is self-destructive.

Friendships may go through ups and downs, but we need friends who will remain loyal to God and to us when all is said and done. Proverbs 12:26 says, "The righteous should choose his friends carefully, for the way of the wicked leads them astray." Do your friends help draw you closer to God, or do they push you away from God? That simple question can go a long way toward filling your life with positive relationships.

The best way to avoid people who are stumbling blocks or betrayers or hateful is to nurture a handful of rich friendships with people who are sold out to God. If they are loyal to Him, they will be loyal to you. And they will lift you up, not tear you down.

Stay Focused on Your Purpose

What did Jesus do when He knew Judas had left the Upper Room to inform officials of His whereabouts? He could've been disheartened and given up, but Jesus knew He still had work to do before His arrest. In the midst of betrayal, Jesus remained focused on His purpose.

Later on, after He was arrested because of Judas' betrayal, Jesus remained steady in the work before Him. He didn't let that betrayal derail Him. Instead, He continued forward, even to the cross. Hebrews 12:2 says of Jesus, "For the joy that was set before Him endured the cross, despising the shame, and has sat down at the right hand of the throne of God."

When you face personal betrayal, choose to focus not on yourself but on your purpose. Just like Jesus, choose to live above the mindset of bitterness and revenge by pouring your life into the work God has called you to achieve. If you stay focused on your purpose, you will be able to keep the pain in perspective.

Pursue Loyalty

Loyalty and commitment are often unpopular because they require us to think of others rather than ourselves. We are selfish at the very core of our fallen nature. But the beauty found in loyalty can counterbalance the awful bitterness of betrayal. We see evidence of that beauty in Revelation 2:10: "Do not fear any of those things which you are about to suffer. Indeed, the devil is about to throw some of you into prison, that you may be tested, and you will have tribulation ten days. Be faithful until death, and I will give you the crown of life."

In a world of betrayal, let's pursue the kind of loyalty that inspires others to remain faithful in their commitment to Christ. Don't falter or give up in doing good and staying true. Keep pressing on without losing the power of resolution.

Do Good to Those Who Hate You

How are we to specifically respond to those betray us, especially those who claim to be Christians? This is one of those questions to which the

Bible gives a simple answer: We are to show love and do good to those who harm us. The Bible couldn't be any clearer on this matter. Consider Paul's words to the Romans: "Bless those who persecute you; bless and do not curse. . . . Do not repay anyone evil for evil. Be careful to do what is right in the eyes of everyone. If it is possible, as far as it depends on you, live at peace with everyone. Do not take revenge, my dear friends, but leave room for God's wrath, for it is written: 'It is mine to avenge; I will repay,' says the Lord" (Romans 12:14, 17–19 NIV).

Count on the Character of God

Finally, the best way to deal with betrayal is to lean on the sovereignty and the love of God. When Paul was sold out by Alexander the copper-smith, he pressed on to write his final letter (see 2 Timothy) with the resolution of finishing his race and keeping the faith: "But the Lord stood with me and strengthened me, so that the message might be preached fully through me, and that all the Gentiles might hear. Also I was delivered out of the mouth of the lion. And the Lord will deliver me from every evil work and preserve me for His heavenly kingdom" (2 Timothy 4:17–18).

Perhaps the key to processing the betrayal we experience as followers of Jesus is reckoning that for every person who deserts us, God has blessed us abundantly more with His never-ceasing faithfulness. Our Savior will never leave us nor forsake us. His loyalty is as immeasurable as His love. His overruling sovereignty will eventually turn our moments of bitterness into occasions for praise. Count on it!

There is no betrayal, pain, or heartache that can keep God from accomplishing His work through us and for us. As the Bible says, "For I am persuaded that neither death nor life, nor angels nor principalities nor powers, nor things present nor things to come, nor height nor depth, nor any other created thing, shall be able to separate us from the love of God which is in Christ Jesus our Lord" (Romans 8:38–39).

Let us learn the value of loyalty in an age of treachery. And let it always be said that followers of Jesus are faithful and true—even in a world full of betrayal and deceit. Don't let such a world trip you up or drag you down. Instead, be faithful to the One who will never leave us nor forsake us.

APPLICATION

Personal Questions

1. Read Matthew 24:10. What is predicted by Jesus?

2. Why do you think we will experience betrayal on a greater scale during the World of the End?

3. What makes betrayal painful? Have you ever been betrayed? If so, how did it make you feel?

4. What was the first act of betrayal, according to the Bible (see Ezekiel 28:14 NLT; Isaiah 14:12–17)? Can you think of any other acts of betrayal in the Bible? List them below.

5. Read Luke 22:3–5.

    a. Who betrayed Jesus (see verse 3)?

b. For what did Judas betray Jesus (see verse 5)?

c. How does this betrayal of Judas compare to the betrayal of God by Satan in Ezekiel 28:14? In what ways are these two betrayals different, if any?

d. When you hear the name *Judas*, what do you immediately think of? What has it become a synonym for?

6. Why do you think Christians will betray other Christians, according to this prophecy?

7. From this lesson, what are the three categories within the prophecy of betrayal? Write them down, and then define them in your own words.

8. As followers of Christ, how should we respond to betrayal?

Group Questions

1. As a group, define the term *betrayal*.

2. Have you ever been betrayed by someone close to you? If so, share with the group. How did it make you feel? How did you respond?

3. What are some of the biggest betrayals found in the Bible?

   a. Who betrayed God (see Ezekiel 28:14 NLT; Isaiah 14:12–17)?

   b. Who betrayed Jesus (see Luke 22:3–5)?

4. Read 1 Timothy 1:20 and 2 Timothy 4:14–15. Discuss how Paul might have been betrayed by Alexander the coppersmith and Paul's warning to Timothy about Alexander.

5. Why do betrayal and hatred often go hand in hand?

6. Read Matthew 24:10. Why would Jesus warn us, His followers, about betrayal from within the Church?

7. Why do you think true Christians are the object, instead of the source, of hatred and betrayal? Discuss.

8. What are some ways that we can maintain unity and fellowship within the Church? Share your ideas.

9. What should our response be to betrayal?

10. According to this lesson, what are five ways in which we can be prepared for being betrayed? In other words, how can we prevent it?

DID YOU KNOW?

One of the greatest acts of betrayal in the Bible is found in the pages of its first book, specifically Genesis 37. Think of how Joseph felt when his own brothers stripped off his colorful robe, threw him in a cistern, and sold him into slavery. Could there be a more painful act of betrayal than having your own family sell you into a life of torture and imprisonment? But when Joseph had the chance to retaliate years later, he did not. Instead, he acknowledged that even though his brothers' actions were intended for evil, God took them and miraculously transformed them for good.

Notes

1. History.com editors, "Robert Hanssen, FBI agent turned Russian spy, is sentenced to life in prison," *HISTORY*, May 9, 2022, https://www.history.com/this-day-in-history/robert-hanssen-fbi-russian-spy-sentenced.
2. Louis J. Freeh, "Veteran FBI Agent Arrested and Charged with Espionage," *FBI.gov*, February 21, 2001, https://archives.fbi.gov/archives/news/pressrel/press-releases/veteran-fbi-agent-arrested-and-charged-with-espionage.
3. Les Parrott, *High-Maintenance Relationships* (Wheaton, IL: Tyndale House Publishers, 1996), 95.
4. Gordon Fee, *1 & 2 Timothy, Titus* (Grand Rapids, MI: Baker Book House, 1988), 4-5, 296.

IN A WORLD OF LAWLESSNESS, BE KIND

MATTHEW 24:12

In this lesson we look at how society collapses when law and order are no longer heeded.

The Golden Rule has been a de facto governing principle of respectable societies for centuries. The thinking has been that if a majority of people treated each other in the manner in which they would like to be treated, a somewhat harmonious existence would be possible. And up to a certain point it has been that way in our communities. But now lawlessness has gained a foothold in modern culture.

OUTLINE

I. The World of Lawlessness
    A. Wickedness Will Increase
    B. Love Will Grow Cold

II. The Way of Kindness
   A. Embrace God's Kindness
   B. Express God's Kindness
   C. Embody God's Kindness

OVERVIEW

Most of us who have grown up in America and the West have felt relatively safe. We have had access to law enforcement agencies and emergency response systems populated by millions of good and decent people. We have elected leaders who swore to uphold laws designed to create a peaceful society. We have lived in relative peace.

But lately, something has changed. Our police officers have been so vilified by the media that they find it difficult to do their jobs. And when they do enforce the law, they are affronted and attacked by the populace.

Moreover, the laws designed to create a harmonious society are outright ignored, and instead our streets are marked by violence, rioting, and homelessness. What has happened to us?

The answer lies in what Jesus predicted in the Olivet Discourse: "And because lawlessness will abound, the love of many will grow cold" (Matthew 24:12). Our society is becoming less loving and more violent. It is simply a symptom of the countdown to the end of the age.

The World of Lawlessness

Before we look at what an anarchistic society looks like, let's review the sequence of events that will take place before the Rapture of the Church, all the while remembering the birth pains principle—these same events will continue to accelerate in frequency and intensity during the Tribulation.

Before the time of the Rapture, deceivers will come upon the scene in a strong way. Wars and rumors of wars will rage. Famines, plagues, and earthquakes will increase in size and scope. The world authorities will track down Christians with persecution spreading to all corners of the globe.

Believers in Christ will face betrayal and hatred, and many false prophets will rise up and deceive multitudes.

With this cascading torrent of crises, it's not surprising to learn that violence will increase during this period and that love will proportionally decrease. Yet, there's an even deeper reality behind these trends. All these events represent a collective rejection of Jesus Christ on this planet. This is the fulfillment of Psalm 2, which is quoted seven times in the New Testament, including in the book of Revelation. "Why do the nations conspire and the peoples plot in vain? The kings of the earth rise up and the rulers band together against the Lord and against His anointed, saying, 'Let us break their chains and throw off their shackles'" (Psalm 2:1–3 NIV).

Everything that Jesus said will occur is only going to widen the distance between humanity and heaven. Nations will intentionally abandon the values and priorities prescribed in Scripture that led to their prosperity. Cultures will uncouple from the biblically grounded institutions that have provided the safety, security, and success we have taken for granted for so many years.

Look again at Matthew 24:12: "And *because* lawlessness will abound, the love of many will grow cold" (emphasis added). The word "because" implies a cause-and-effect relationship between the two clauses of that sentence. As people reject the justice that comes from God's righteousness, they will forfeit the love that comes from His grace. This begins a vicious downward cycle, almost like a tornado of chaos. Lawlessness begets lovelessness, and lovelessness produces more lawlessness.

Wickedness Will Increase

When Jesus said, "Lawlessness will abound," He was describing more than the absence of laws or law enforcement. His words call to mind periods of human history that were defined by chaos and disorder. Think of the terrible plight of the Dark Ages or the bloody legacy of two world wars in the first half of the twentieth century. However, the lawlessness Jesus points to in the End Times will be exponentially worse than anything we've witnessed before.

Biblical scholar Frederick Dale Bruner describes this future period as a season of "unique lawlessness" in which the very concept of morality will be turned upside down. Right and wrong will be inverted, with entire cultures celebrating what is evil and condemning what is good. Bruner wrote, "Sinful human beings always practice lawlessness, but there will be a unique lawlessness at the end. Good will be called evil and evil will be called good on a massive and unprecedented scale, exponentially... People will 'glory in their shame.'"[1]

As society moves ever closer to the World of the End, we can feel the currents of the Tribulation blowing backward into our own atmosphere. As never before, we need to be able to articulate biblical positions on moral issues without confusing or reversing right and wrong. We also need to understand that the growing insanity in our world isn't primarily a political or military problem—it is a spiritual problem. The further our world strays from Christ, the closer it will drift toward cruelty and chaos.

Love Will Grow Cold

This growing wickedness and lawlessness will also cause the "love of many [to] grow cold." The New International Version says, "The love of most will grow cold" (24:12). Not just *many* people, but *most* people! The further we drift from God's justice, the less we will reflect God's love. Anger begets anger.

Years ago, a cartoon appeared in the paper showing four panels. In the first, a boss was chewing out an employee. In the next, the employee was coming home and snapping at his wife. The third panel showed the wife chewing out the young son. And in the last panel, the boy was kicking the dog. Anger can produce a chain reaction that can travel quickly, and we never know where the violence will erupt next.

As wickedness grows, the love of most people "will grow cold." That very phrase is a translation of the Greek root word *psycho*, which literally means "to breathe or blow." This is the source of our English words *psyche* and *psychology*. This usually implies a living person, human spirit, or soul.

But in Matthew 24:12, the word is used more in the context of blowing air across something. Think of your coffee when it is too hot to drink. What do you do? You blow on it, allowing the air to stir the top of the liquid, cooling it just a bit. That's the picture Jesus utilized in the Olivet Discourse. As the wind of lawlessness blows across our world, it chills our love, and the world becomes a colder place.

The Way of Kindness

It is difficult to watch the world disconnect from God. Society's slide toward lawlessness and lovelessness is painful and produces real consequences. We personally feel a jolt when outside forces corrupt the institutions and customs we have cherished for so long. Darkness seems to be deepening over our culture like the edge of night.

But we are not powerless! Philippians 2:15–16 says that we are "children of God without fault in the midst of a crooked and perverse generation, among whom [we] shine as lights in the world, holding fast the word of life." We should not sit back passively as humanity turns its back on God's justice and God's love. Yes, the trends are going in the wrong direction as we approach the End Times, but the Church is still on earth, and we can still make a difference!

We have limited ability to control the lawlessness and lovelessness in our society, but we can control how we respond to those factors. Specifically, we can use those realities as opportunities to advance God's Kingdom prior to the end of history. Here are three specific ways we can reflect God's kindness in a culture of wickedness—and keep our love for God and for one another from growing cold when lawlessness abounds.

Embrace God's Kindness

Before we can demonstrate God's love and kindness to people in the world, we need to embrace that love and kindness for ourselves. Maybe you've not received the human love you needed. Perhaps you've been abused, neglected, or mistreated. We all battle issues of self-worth, and everyone wonders at some point whether God loves them. You may feel all alone.

If only you knew how crazy God is about you! He really loves you! It's our being loved by God that makes us different. His love isn't mere emotion; it is the very essence of who He is.

People who possess that knowledge of God's love are insulated from the chilling winds that can cause warm affection to become hard ice. When we embrace the love of God through Christ, our own love will not grow cold. That is why Paul reminded the earliest believers in Romans 5:5, "The love of God has been poured out in our hearts by the Holy Spirit who was given to us."

On a practical level, our sense of God's love deepens as we spend time with Him. How do spend time with Him? By setting aside time for private prayer. By studying His Word. By worshiping Him publicly and privately. These are the habits that can keep the love of God simmering in our hearts. It is very hard for your love to grow cold when the fervent love of God is surging through your veins.

Express God's Kindness

When we embrace God's love, it becomes natural to express His love. Nothing is more obvious in the Bible than God's commands to love the world in tangible ways, and in many ways, kindness is God's love expressed through action. This isn't just a call for a select few followers of Jesus; it is for all Christians. Psalm 82:3 says, "Defend the poor and fatherless; do justice to the afflicted and needy."

Jesus put it like this: "He who has two tunics, let him give to him who has none; and he who has food, let him do likewise" (Luke 3:11). In like manner, James said, "Pure and undefiled religion before God and the Father is this: to visit orphans and widows in their trouble" (James 1:27).

Expressing God's kindness can mean fulfilling these commands in both big and small ways. It can be as simple as raking a neighbor's yard or as serious as taking care of an aging parent or helping a friend walk through an addiction. The point is that we do something! God's love is not about warm thoughts or well-wishes—it is expressed through action.

Embody God's Kindness

How do we reflect God's kindness in a world increasingly defined by lawlessness? First, by embracing God's love daily so that it fills us up. Second, by intentionally expressing that love to others through regular action. Third, as we encounter God's love in greater degrees—both receiving and giving—we embody that love. In other words, we need to make God's love become part of our very identity.

A young man named Hunter Shamatt caught a glimpse of that solution after he flew to Las Vegas for his sister's wedding. When he arrived at the hotel, he realized he'd lost his wallet. More than that, he'd lost the $60 cash, $400 signed paycheck, ID, and bank card that were inside his wallet. The young man tried to maintain a brave face throughout the festivities celebrating his sister, but he was devastated. He needed that money.

Then, to his very great surprise, Hunter received a package the day after he returned home. Inside was his wallet. And inside the wallet was his bank card, ID, $400 signed paycheck—and not $60 cash, but $100! There was also a note that read: "Hunter, found this on a Frontier flight from Omaha to Denver—row 12, seat F wedged between the seat and wall. Thought you might want it back. All the best. P.S. I rounded your cash up to an even $100 so you could celebrate getting your wallet back. Have fun!!!"

After reading the note, Hunter was dumbfounded. "No way," he kept saying. "That can't be. Just no way."[2]

That is a mundane story when compared with the grand scope of history, but it offers a picture of what it means to embody God's love. What if you and I were to reflect God's love to such a degree that the world around us felt astounded or even dumbfounded? What kind of difference could we make if we achieved that level of kindness in a world afflicted on every side by wickedness?

Jesus gave us another picture of what it means to embody God's love, and I want to introduce it by walking you through a little exercise. Take a moment to mentally transport yourself back to the ancient world of Jesus' day. It is late in the evening, and the sun has set. The last light of day is fading from the night sky. You have been walking for more than ten hours under the heat of that sun. You are tired, sore, hungry, and eager for an end to a long day.

Then you see it: a glimmering light in the distance. After another few minutes of walking, that light becomes the welcoming glow of a city built next to the road on the side of a hill. The light you see is not produced by wires and bulbs, but by cookfires and hearths and oil lamps hanging on doorposts. There are people in that city. There is water there to wash the grime off your feet. There is even a bed to recline on after you take your evening meal.

As a weary traveler, can you imagine anything warmer and more wonderful in that moment? Could you stumble upon anything more welcoming and refreshing?

This is the very image that Jesus used to describe how His Church should shine the light of the Gospel to the world: "You are the light of the world. A city that is set on a hill cannot be hidden. Nor do they light a lamp and put it under a basket, but on a lampstand, and it gives light to all who are in the house. Let your light so shine before men, that they may see your good works and glorify your Father in heaven" (Matthew 5:14–16).

Here's a simple principle—light shines brightest in the darkness. And in a world frozen from lawlessness and lack of love, we have the unique opportunity to radiate the radical warmth of the Gospel. We also have the opportunity to radiate the warmth of community, the warmth of fellowship, and the warmth of intimacy with our Creator to a cold and dark world.

Though we have limited control over the dire trends of lawlessness and lovelessness in our culture, we can control how we respond personally to those realities. We can choose to display forgiveness rather than bitterness. We can choose to heal rather than harm, to help rather than hurt. We can choose to be welcoming witnesses when everyone else practices the emotional equivalent of social distancing. In short, we can choose to be God's love.

It is true that our world has lost something important. We have drifted far away from God's justice and love. Actually, we haven't drifted—we've defected! Humanity is in the process of intentionally rejecting its Creator, and the future looks beyond bleak.

But you and I have an opportunity to capitalize on those losses. We can show the world what they are missing. We can take a stand for goodness and love and return what has been so badly lost, even if it is only for a season. As we do so, we can add that little extra gift that makes all the difference to a dying world—an extra serving of God's love.

The breakdown of law and order is like a deadly wind blowing across our nation and world, chilling the love of many people. But the fire of God's love can keep us warm and impassioned for Christ as we wait for His return.

We are to embrace God's kindness, express God's kindness, and embody God's kindness. Those are our marching orders in a society that is ever tilting towards anarchy. You can still make a difference for Christ in this crazy world. You can be the difference in someone's life that keeps their heart open to God's love. In so doing, you and I can achieve what the early Christians did—turning the world upside down. Choose to be kind today!

APPLICATION

Personal Questions

1. Read Matthew 24:12.

    a. What is your first takeaway from this verse?

    b. What kind of "lawlessness" was Jesus speaking of?

    c. Why would Jesus say that the "love of many will grow cold" in His Olivet Discourse?

    d. How do lawlessness and a lack of love go hand in hand?

    e. Do you think this lawlessness and lack of love we will experience in the World of the End are due to an abandonment of the Scriptures? Why or why not?

2. For what reason(s) will our society start becoming lawless? Would you say we are already seeing our society become lawless? If so, in what ways?

3. What will be the consequences to society for endorsing lawlessness instead of the Scriptures?

4. Biblically speaking, how are we to address love in a lawless world?

5. Read Philippians 2:15–16. How does this passage describe "children of God"?

6. Are we, as Christians, still able to make a difference in how we respond to lawlessness and lovelessness? In what manner?

7. Based on this lesson, describe how we can reflect God's kindness.

8. How can you personally keep your love for God and for others from growing cold?

Group Questions

1. Define the term *lawlessness* based on the lesson. Does it only mean to break laws or is the definition broader in terms of culture and how we treat others? Share your ideas with the group.

2. Read Matthew 24:12 together.

   a. Why would Jesus tell us that "lawlessness will abound"?

   b. In what ways will lawlessness increase?

   c. What does the word "because" indicate? Is there a correlation be-
      tween lawlessness abounding and the "love of many [growing] cold"?
      If so, explain.

3. Read Psalm 2:1–3 as a group. For what reason will lawlessness increase?

4. What does love in a lawless world look like? How should we respond to it
   (see Philippians 2:15–16)?

5. How can we understand, communicate, and exemplify the Bible as society moves closer to the World of the End? Discuss as a group.

6. What happens when we embrace God's kindness for us? What becomes natural to us?

7. As a group, what does embracing, expressing, and embodying God's kindness look like?

8. How can we reflect God's love in such a way that it will dumbfound the world around us?

DID YOU KNOW?

The prophet Isaiah lived in a tumultuous time. During his life, the wicked and evil nation of Assyria was at full power and laid much abuse on Israel, God's chosen people. Amid threats to the life and liberty of his own people, Isaiah offered up a foreshadowing of the season of lawlessness that we now face thousands of years later: "Woe to those who call evil good, and good evil; who put darkness for light, and light for darkness; who put bitter for sweet, and sweet for bitter! Woe to those who are wise in their own eyes, and prudent in their own sight!" (Isaiah 5:20–21)

Notes

1. Frederick Dale Bruner, *Matthew: A Commentary—Volume 2: The Churchbook: Matthew 13–28* (Grand Rapids, MI: William B. Eerdmans Publishing Company, 2004), Kindle Edition.
2. Allison Klein, "Lost wallet returned, with something extra inside," *The Washington Post*, November 27, 2018, https://www.washingtonpost.com/lifestyle/2018/11/27/lost-wallet-returned-with-something-extra-inside/.

IN A WORLD OF BAD NEWS, BE THE GOOD NEWS

MATTHEW 24:14

In this lesson we see that the Gospel of Jesus Christ will be unstoppable as the world nears its end.

Television news stations thrive by televising and commenting on the horrors of the day, which are many. When our minds are filled with the bad news, it's easy to become downtrodden with the state of society. But at every time in history, and especially now, the Gospel is a bright light shining in a dark world.

OUTLINE

I. **The Unstoppable Message of the Gospel: To the End of the Age**
   A. The Unstoppable Message of the Gospel Before the Rapture
   B. The Unstoppable Message of the Gospel After the Rapture

II. **The Unstoppable Messengers of the Gospel: To the Ends of the Earth**
   A. In Showing
   B. In Sharing
   C. In Supporting

OVERVIEW

Remarkably, on one of the last days of His natural life, Jesus predicted a time when the Gospel of the Kingdom would be preached to the ends of the earth, heralding the approach of His return. No one in those days could have conceived of such a thing. Jesus of Nazareth was a country preacher in the rural mountains of Galilee. He spoke in simple parables and pastoral teachings, and few people outside His personal circles even knew about Him.

Yet speaking privately with His disciples shortly before His brutal death, He said that one day His unique message would touch the furthest corners of the globe. It would go to the ends of the earth—and when it did, the world would be near its end. In Matthew 24:14, Jesus said, "And this gospel of the kingdom will be preached in all the world as a witness to all the nations, and then the end will come."

Of all of Jesus' statements that we have studied thus far in Matthew 24, this one is the most implausible. Predicting worldwide war and plagues is intense but not implausible. Calling out the rise and fall of religious deceivers makes some sense. But who would predict that the words of a rural rabbi from Galilee would reverberate in every subsequent generation and still be life-changing two thousand years later?

But this was our Lord's positive prediction! So far, we have looked at a lot of grim prognostications in the Olivet Discourse. But during all those difficult days at the end of history, one thing will be unstoppable: the relentless spread of the Gospel of Jesus Christ. The Gospel will be preached to every generation, on every continent, and through every difficult circumstance. Like a beam of light through the blackened night, the Good News will bring the world its only hope. The message of Jesus—crucified and resurrected—will echo through all the turbulence of time and herald His swift return.

The Unstoppable Message of the Gospel: To the End of the Age

Let's start out by defining the word *gospel*. The Greek term for *gospel* in the New Testament is *evangelion*. Obviously, this is the source of the word *evangelism*. But look closer. Notice the middle letters: *ev-angel-ion*. What is an *angel* doing in the middle of the Gospel? The word *angel* means "messenger." The Greek prefix *ev* means "good." So the word *gospel* means "good message" or "good news."

This term first appears in the Bible at the beginning of Jesus' ministry. In Matthew 4:23 we read, "And Jesus went about all Galilee, teaching in their synagogues, preaching the gospel of the kingdom, and healing all kinds of sickness and all kinds of disease among the people."

The Gospel is the set of historical facts relating to the death and resurrection of Jesus Christ. It includes the eternal repercussions of those facts for those who place their faith in Christ. Through Jesus, man can enter a living relationship with God, by grace and through faith. Christ alone offers us all forgiveness of sin and the hope of eternal life.

Ephesians 1:13 says, "In [Christ] you also trusted, after you heard the word of truth, the [good news] of your salvation." The word *good* seems like the world's greatest understatement. Our culture loves superlative terms like *amazing*, *awesome*, and *spectacular*. To us today, *good* is far down on that list of adjectives.

But the Bible uses *good* as both a moral quality of God and as a way to describe the nature of the gifts He has given us. In His vocabulary, *good* is far beyond amazing, awesome, and spectacular. It may be His highest adjective! We can pack every superlative we want into those four letters—GOOD—and there will still be an eternity of room left over.

The Gospel was sealed and settled by Jesus' shed blood at Calvary and His glorious resurrection. Evangelist D. L. Moody said, "The most solemn truth in the gospel is that the only thing Christ left down here is His blood."[1] When we receive this message by simple faith and confess Christ as Lord of our lives, we become living recipients and embodiments of the Good News. In other words, we say "Yes" to Jesus.

Going back to Matthew 24:14, there is something else to notice. The verse says, "And this gospel of the kingdom will be preached." Why is it called the "gospel of the kingdom"? The answer can sound complicated, but it's a simple concept. The word *kingdom* is short for the "king's domain." Except for once, every time Matthew used the word *Gospel*, he couched it in that phrase "gospel of the kingdom."

There is a famous theological phrase that says our Lord's Kingdom is "already but not yet." When Jesus came to our world the first time, He planted the Kingdom of believers on this planet, placing the foundation for His Church. Colossians 1:13 says, "He has delivered us from the power of darkness and conveyed us into the kingdom of the Son of His love."

When Christ comes again, He will establish His theocratic Kingdom in Israel and reign from there for a thousand years. So, in one sense, Jesus' Kingdom is already here. But in another sense, it is still to be established—"already but not yet."

In Mark's version of the Olivet Discourse, Jesus is recorded as simply saying, "And the gospel must first be preached to all the nations" (Mark 13:10). That's the key point! Both the current Kingdom of the Church and the coming Kingdom of the Millennial Age spring from the historical fact of Jesus' death and resurrection. The same Gospel that makes you and me instant members of God's heavenly Kingdom right now will also be the power plant allowing Christ to rule the world after His return to earth.

The Unstoppable Message of the Gospel Before the Rapture

The first verses of the Olivet Discourse carry an "already but not yet" flavor. They describe the days leading up to the Rapture of the Church. They then rewind and take us through the same general sequence of events during the first half of the Tribulation with a deeper level of judgment and distress.

On one level, the Lord Jesus was predicting the deterioration of world events during the periods leading to the Rapture. These are the times we are experiencing now. As we have already covered, this will be a time of increasing danger from deceivers, wars, international conflict, famine, pandemics, and natural disasters. Persecution will spike around the world, and love will fade away as a uniting force.

But the one positive trend amidst these bleak signs is the Good News: "And this gospel of the kingdom will be preached in all the world as a witness to all the nations, and then the end will come" (Matthew 24:14). The end of what? The end of the Church Age! The presence of the Spirit-indwelled Church will be removed from this planet in a flash of time. Graves will become launching pads, and believers will fly into the clouds to be instantly transformed with glorified bodies.

No one listening to Jesus that day on Olivet could have imagined this prediction coming true. Yet Jesus repeated this claim in Acts 1:8, telling His disciples: "But you shall receive power when the Holy Spirit has come upon you; and you shall be witnesses to Me in Jerusalem, and in all Judea and Samaria, and to the end of the earth."

Shortly after, on the Day of Pentecost, three thousand people confessed Christ in Jerusalem and were baptized (see Acts 2:41). Many of them then went home from the festival of Pentecost and took the message of Jesus to provinces, cities, towns, and islands throughout the Roman Empire. Soon the number of believers reached five thousand (see Acts 4:4). The disciples began multiplying exponentially (see Acts 6:1), and the number of churches multiplied as well (see Acts 9:31).

From Antioch, the first official church-sent missionaries were commissioned: Barnabas and Paul. The age of organized missions then began, and by the early 300s, the Roman Empire had already been reshaped by the Gospel. But the spreading of the Gospel is not limited to just that period in history.

Every generation of Christians has spread the Good News to those around them. Yes, there have been some giants in the list of missionaries and evangelists: Patrick, Wesley, Carey, Moody, and Graham. But most of the work has been accomplished by people like you and me who share our testimonies in the same way mariners tell the stories of their rescues from shipwrecks.

Where are we today in world evangelism? The Joshua Project keeps careful track of what God is doing on the earth. According to their research, there are 17,427 people groups on earth, and about 10,000 have been reached with the Gospel. There are still 7,414 groups needing the Gospel, and many of those are in very restricted nations.[2] That's the bad news.

The good news is that today we're starting to penetrate even the most difficult barriers by means of new technology. The Internet is essential, of course. But cheaper methods for setting up satellite TV and radio programs have also allowed preachers to reach directly into the homes of those interested to learn more about Christ, even when those homes are in countries actively hostile to the Gospel.

We are seeing the fulfillment of Jesus' prophecy in real time: The Gospel is being preached throughout all the world as a witness to all nations and all peoples. When that process is complete, the stage will be set for Jesus to return once and for all.

The Unstoppable Message of the Gospel After the Rapture

The events prophesied in Matthew 24:1–14 will back up and replay after the Rapture of the Church, but at a higher volume and with greater intensity. After believers vanish from the earth, there will be a new round of deceivers, including the Man of Lawlessness (the Antichrist). This will be an unprecedented time of war and rumors of war.

Nation will rise against nation and kingdom against kingdom. As seen in the breaking of the seven seals in Revelation 6, there will be famines, pestilences, and earthquakes in various places. All these events lead up to the middle of the Tribulation and to the terrible period known as the Great Tribulation.

But many people don't realize that the first half of the Tribulation will be one of the greatest evangelistic awakenings in human history. The Gospel will be unstoppable then! You may ask, "If the church is removed, who will be evangelizing?"

Perhaps the greatest distribution of Bibles in history occurred during World War I, with multiple Bible societies printing New Testaments and getting them into the hands of millions of soldiers. One report said, "Soldiers, when they were very badly wounded, had a tendency to produce the New Testament from their breast pocket and read it as they died. This is a phenomenon that was recorded when soldiers who were killed on 1 July 1916—the first day of the Battle of the Somme—were recovered and buried, many of them were found dead with the Bible, or New Testament in their hands."[3]

Could that be a preview of the Tribulation?

In addition, the Lord is going to commission 144,000 Jewish evangelists who will spread the Gospel with the zeal of the apostle Paul to the ends of the earth (see Revelation 7:1–4). Everyone converted under their ministries will also reach others, and many of them will be martyred (see Revelation 7:9–17). And don't forget the two super-evangelists the Lord will place in Jerusalem, described in Revelation 11!

The Unstoppable Messengers of the Gospel: To the Ends of the Earth

The unstoppable message of the Gospel will be (and is being) spread by unstoppable messengers. In our generation, that means that you and I are to take the Gospel to the ends of the earth. Jesus predicted His followers would be unstoppable in taking His Gospel to the world, but how do we do it? Here are three ways to share the uncontainable Good News.

In Showing

Our most basic testimony has to do with our lives—daily exhibiting a biblical lifestyle in this ungodly age. That requires a constant walk with the Lord, a desire for personal holiness, a growing attitude of Christlikeness, and a burden to love others and meet their needs in Jesus' Name.

Does your life so exhibit Jesus Christ that others can see the Gospel in you—in your attitudes, activities, demeanor, integrity, and love? The apostle Peter said in 1 Peter 3:15–16, "But in your hearts revere Christ as Lord. Always be prepared to give an answer to everyone who asks you to give the reason for the hope that you have. But do this with gentleness and respect, keeping a clear conscience, so that those who speak maliciously against your good behavior in Christ may be ashamed of their slander" (NIV).

Live in a way that reflects the power of the Gospel, and always be ready to share the message of the Gospel when opportunities arise. Those are two principles that can have an eternal impact on those you encounter. It's really as simple as that. As we look for opportunities and think of others more than ourselves, the Lord lets us come alongside others and influence them.

In Sharing

At some point in sharing our faith, words are necessary. They can be spoken, printed, or even texted on a phone, but people need to know that Christ has died for their sins and is risen from the tomb. They need to hear the Good News of salvation that is found in Jesus, the Son of God.

At some point, we have to communicate these truths to others. That is why 2 Timothy 4:5 says, "Do the work of an evangelist." Remember that Greek word, *evangelion*? The word with an *angel* in the middle of it, meaning "messenger"? The Bible is telling you to be a Good News messenger. And doing so doesn't require a theological degree, just a willingness to share your faith.

Whom can you reach? Ask God to open a door for you to share your faith. Practice your testimony. Learn some verses that summarize the Gospel, such as Romans 6:23: "For the wages of sin is death, but the gift of God is eternal life in Christ Jesus our Lord." Cast out fear, and don't be afraid of failure. Trust God to give you the right words at the right time, and then leave the results to Him.

In Supporting

We can also share the Gospel by sharing our resources for the expansion of the Kingdom. When we regularly and prayerfully give our tithes and offerings to our local church, the Lord transmutes them into tangible works of grace. The Philippians provided financial support for Paul's journeys, and his success became their success.

Pastor Chuck Sligh told of a missionary who "returned to England for a brief furlough after many years of faithful service in India. He was invited to a dinner at a great summer resort where he met many women of prominence and position. After dinner he went to his room and penned a letter to his wife. He wrote, 'My Dearest Sweetheart: I've had dinner at the hotel. The company was wonderful. I saw strange things today. Many women were present. There were some who, to my certain knowledge, wore one church, forty cottage organs, twenty libraries and 30,000 Bibles.'"

This man, in his intense longing to provide the Gospel to the spiritually hungry millions in India, "could not refrain from estimating the silks, satins, and diamonds of the guests at the dinner in terms of his people's needs on the mission field."[4]

That is a good illustration as long as we don't let it "guilt" us into giving. Our silver and gold will perish, but those we win to Christ will join us in heaven forever.

We are living in the Last Days, and we are the only ones who have good news for this world! The media doesn't. Academia doesn't. The entertainment industry doesn't. The politicians and statesmen certainly don't have anything positive to offer.

The only place where hope is found is in the proclamation of the Good News by the followers of Jesus. And today, people all over the globe are risking their lives to share it.

What a privilege, then, for us to show the Gospel, to share it, and to support it. The message of the Gospel is unstoppable, continuing to the end of the age. And the messengers of the Gospel are unstoppable, going to the end of the world. That is why we can't stop the work we have been given to do until the Lord takes us home.

People need the Lord. Our world has never needed Him more. So, let's all be evangelists for Christ wherever we go, whatever the cost, until everyone on earth has heard the Good News of Jesus.

APPLICATION

Personal Questions

1. Read Matthew 24:14.

   a. How do you think the Gospel will be preached "in all the world"?

   b. Who will preach the Gospel?

   c. Why will the Gospel be known as "a witness"?

   d. How does Mark 13:10 relate to Matthew 24:14?

2.   How does the New Testament define the term *Gospel*?

3.   Specifically, to whom will the Gospel be preached?

4.   What will happen after the Gospel is preached throughout the world?

5.   Describe what is meant by the Lord's Kingdom being "already but not yet."

6.   How would you explain the Good News to nonbelievers?

7. By what methods can we preach the Gospel today? How has technology helped us spread the Good News at faster rates than ever before?

8. What is the mission of the Gospel? How will it be unstoppable during the Tribulation?

9. Currently, who are the unstoppable messengers of the Gospel?

10. Based on this lesson, what are three ways we can share the Good News of the Gospel with others?

Group Questions

1. Read Matthew 24:14 and Mark 13:10 together as a group.

   a. What must be preached?

b. What did Jesus mean by the "gospel of the kingdom" in Matthew 24:14?

c. Where must the Gospel first be preached before the return of Christ?

d. Discuss what is meant by the Lord's Kingdom being "already but not yet."

2. According to this lesson, the Greek term for *Gospel* means "good message" or "good news."

a. Why do you think that is?

b. In what ways does the Bible use the word *good*?

3. The Gospel is historical facts relating to the death and resurrection of Jesus Christ. Discuss with the group what this entails and how it affects those who place their faith in Jesus.

4. Discuss how the greatest evangelistic awakening in human history will take place during the first half of the Tribulation.

    a. Who will be evangelizing at this time (see Revelation 7:1–4, 9–17; Revelation 11)?

    b. How will people be evangelizing?

5. Who is to spread the Gospel to our generation?

6. Are you currently living in a way that reflects the power of the Gospel? Why or why not?

7. How can you show, share, and support the Good News? Make a list as
   a group.

DID YOU KNOW?

In Revelation 11:3, we are told of two super-evangelists that the Lord will place in Jerusalem to preach the Gospel: "And I will give power to my two witnesses, and they will prophesy one thousand two hundred and sixty days, clothed in sackcloth." There are many theories as to who these two witnesses may be. Some postulate that it will be the same two Jesus conferred with on the Mount of Transfiguration: Moses and Elijah. Others make the argument that it will be Enoch and Elijah. The truth is, we do not know who these two individuals are, only that they will be powerful in their presentation!

Notes
1. J. B. McClure, *Moody's Anecdotes and Illustrations* (London: Wakefield, 1887), 47.
2. "Global Statistics," *Joshua Project*, accessed June 22, 2022, https://joshuaproject.net/people_groups/statistics.
3. "BBC report highlights importance of Bible to WW1 soldiers," *Bible Society*, May 25, 2021, https://www.biblesociety.org.uk/latest/news/bbc-report-highlights-importance-of-bible-to-ww1-soldiers/.
4. Chuck Sligh, "Why I Want To Have A Big Part In Missions," *Sermon Central*, February 26, 2012, https://www.sermoncentral.com/sermons/why-i-want-to-have-a-big-part-in-missions-chuck-sligh-sermon-on-missions-164924.

IN THE WORLD OF THE END, BE DETERMINED

MATTHEW 24:13

In this lesson we learn how to build up the endurance needed to make it the very end.

Many of us know Aesop's fable, "The Tortoise and the Hare," and were taught as children that slow and steady wins the race. But somehow, through the distractions and disappointments of adulthood, we forgot this simple but powerful lesson. However, this lesson is not just true in the physical realm; it is also true in the spiritual realm. In the Olivet Discourse, Jesus makes it clear that we as Christians are to spiritually endure to the very end, no matter the circumstance.

OUTLINE

I. The Strength of Our Stand

II. The Stamina of Our Stand
   A. Perennial Stamina
   B. Personal Stamina

III. The Satisfaction of Our Stand
    A. What This Salvation Is Not
    B. What This Salvation Is

IV. The Start of Our Stand
    A. Determine to Run Your Race
    B. Determine to React with Radiance
    C. Determine to Reach Your Goal

OVERVIEW

One morning three friends, Charlie Engle, Ray Zahab, and Kevin Lin, began to run across the Sahara Desert from the Atlantic Ocean off the coast of Senegal to the Red Sea. Their route took them through six different nations. They endured blazing temperatures, sandstorms, government corruption, and dangerous conditions. Finally, after 111 days of averaging almost 40 miles a day, the men accomplished their goal and reached the Red Sea.[1]

If you're like me, the first question that comes to mind is, "Why would someone attempt something so audacious and outrageous?" The answer can be found in a single word—*endurance*. If you were to look through various dictionaries, you could find many definitions for the concept of endurance. But I don't think any would be better than this simple statement: You keep going.

That is what it means to endure, and that's what Jesus communicated to His disciples on the Mount of Olives. As we've studied in previous lessons, the "signs of the times" about which Jesus prophesied were frightening for many reasons. He warned about wars and rumors of wars. He spoke about famines and earthquakes and pestilences. He even said that many within the Church would turn their backs on Christ.

But in Matthew 24:13, Jesus offered an incredible promise: "But he who endures to the end shall be saved." That promise was true for Christ's earliest disciples as they endured attacks from the Roman

Empire and the religious leaders within their own community. That promise has been true for all who remained faithful to God's Kingdom throughout history. And that promise is especially critical for believers today as we approach the World of the End.

The Strength of Our Stand

Let's look again at the first part of Jesus' promise: "But he who endures." Scripture is packed with admonitions and encouragements for God's people to "keep going" even when the going gets tough. The Bible uses many terms to describe this quality of our character: *endurance, steadfastness, faithfulness, perseverance*. The basic idea is for followers of Christ to keep following Christ no matter what the circumstance.

In Luke 9:62 Jesus said, "No one, having put his hand to the plow, and looking back, is fit for the kingdom of God." Paul instructed Timothy to keep going in the face of trials: "You therefore must endure hardship as a good soldier of Jesus Christ" (2 Timothy 2:3). A few verses later, he added this: "Therefore I endure all things for the sake of the elect, that they also may obtain the salvation which is in Christ Jesus with eternal glory" (2 Timothy 2:10).

The Greek word translated as "endures" in Matthew 24 is *hupomenó*, which is a combination of *hupo* ("under") and *meno* ("stay" or "remain"). The picture Jesus used to describe "he who endures" is of a person deliberately remaining under a specific directive or command. It's a picture of someone choosing to stay in a certain spot even when everyone else has moved on or moved away.

In our modern vernacular, the term "hang on" is a good synonym for what Jesus was communicating. It takes a lot of strength to hang on. We often think of endurance in connotations of passivity or weakness. For example, a student "endures" a lecture from a teacher. Workers "suffer through" their Thursday and Friday shifts in order to enjoy the weekend. But that is not what Jesus is talking about.

Instead, Jesus' call for endurance is really a command for His followers to take a stand and push against the current. It is a call to refuse to be moved and to hold firm to our Christian convictions even if the whole world is against us. As Paul wrote to the earliest believers:

Finally, my brethren, be strong in the Lord and in the power of His might. Put on the whole armor of God, that you may be able to stand against the wiles of the devil. For we do not wrestle against flesh and blood, but against principalities, against powers, against the rulers of the darkness of this age, against spiritual hosts of wickedness in the heavenly places. Therefore take up the whole armor of God, that you may be able to withstand in the evil day, and having done all, to stand (Ephesians 6:10–13).

The Stamina of Our Stand

Taking a stand for our faith in Christ is the first step necessary for endurance, but it is not the final step. Consider Jesus' words from Matthew 24:13: "But he who endures to the end." That raises a question—the end of what? Is there a specific endpoint we need to reach as followers of Jesus? A specific finish line we need to cross? The answer is both yes and no.

Perennial Stamina

For any believers alive during the final stages of human history, Jesus' words are a call to stand until "the end" of that history—in other words, until His return. For those who will not live to see the end of the world, Jesus' words are a call to endure until "the end" of their respective journeys. Each of us must continue to persevere for as long as necessary.

Personal Stamina

There is an interesting grammatical clue in Matthew 24:13 that highlights the focus of that verse. Up until this point, Jesus had been speaking to His disciples in the plural. He spoke inclusively about the community of Christians at large. But there is a shift in verse 13. The word translated "he" in that verse is the Greek term *ho*, which is singular. "But he [singular] who endures to the end shall be saved."

Accordingly, Jesus was not speaking to the massive audience of the Church when He gave His call to endure "to the end." Instead, He was speaking to you and me as individuals. He was encouraging each one of us to hang on and to keep on hanging on for as long as it takes.

Enduring as a follower of Jesus requires not only strength, but also stamina. We must take our stand for what we know is right and what

God has communicated through His Word. Then we must keep standing no matter what comes our way and no matter how long it takes. We are called to remain steadfast until the very end.

The Satisfaction of Our Stand

Jesus' promise in Matthew 24:13 says, "But he who endures to the end shall be saved." Yes, choosing to endure as followers of Christ will require us to have both strength and stamina, but remaining steadfast will ultimately lead to the salvation of our souls. Let's examine two clarifying points about this powerful promise.

What This Salvation Is Not

Our choice to "endure" in the face of persecution does not produce salvation. I commend every person who takes a stand for Christ, but it is critical for every person to understand that our strength and stamina can never erase the reality of our sin. Instead, "by grace you have been saved through faith, and that not of yourselves; it is the gift of God, not of works, lest anyone should boast" (Ephesians 2:8–9).

When Jesus promised that everyone who "endures to the end shall be saved," He was not guaranteeing that everyone would be removed from the difficulties of the End Times. Far from it! As you know, many believers throughout history made the ultimate sacrifice by standing firm in their faith even unto death. There will be many martyrs for the cause of Christ as we move closer and closer to the end of history.

Taking a stand for Christ is not a "get out of jail free" card. Instead, it is an opportunity to experience the blessing of God's goodness and peace even amid the most challenging circumstances. Just remember this other promise from Jesus found in John 16:33: "In the world you will have tribulation; but be of good cheer, I have overcome the world."

What This Salvation Is

The message of Scripture is clear: Followers of Jesus should expect to experience resistance and persecution. These threats will confront us more and more as we move closer and closer to Jesus' return. And yet we do not need to be afraid. Why? Because as Paul said, "The Lord will rescue me from every evil attack and will bring me safely to his heavenly kingdom. To him be glory forever and ever. Amen" (2 Timothy 4:18 NIV). For those who endure to the end, the Lord will rescue them from evil and bring them safely to His heavenly Kingdom.

The Start of Our Stand

When we consider terms like *endurance* or *perseverance*, it is easy to think of them in terms of tomorrow rather than today. But the determination to follow Christ no matter the cost isn't something we can manifest in a moment. It takes a lifetime to build and to grow into.

Endurance is a choice you and I need to make now. We don't take our stand for Christ only when that stand feels urgent. Rather, the start of our stand begins today. You cannot perform that which you do not practice.

Here are three specific ways you can begin practicing endurance and steadfastness as a follower of Christ. These are choices you and I can make starting today so that we are ready to maintain our stand in the World of the End.

Determine to Run Your Race

We must have a God-given, incontestable, undeniable determination to live for Christ, no matter the cost. In Luke 9:23 Jesus said, "If anyone desires to come after Me, let him deny himself, and take up his cross daily, and follow Me." Make up your mind now that nothing will deter you from God's will, that no one will draw you from His path, that no foe will defeat you, and that no sin will stop you.

Make every moment count. Don't allow yourself to give in or give up when you experience difficulties. Instead, push through and keep working and striving to live for Christ.

Followers of Christ must be prepared to endure trials of various kinds as we seek to finish the race. Jesus Himself promised we would face tribulation. But here is a principle and a promise that can help us keep striving: Those trials and tribulations can become fuel for our endurance. No matter what the world throws our way, we can recycle those experiences through the power of God and transform our pain into power. Consider these two passages from the New Testament.

Count it all joy, my brothers, when you meet trials of various kinds, for you know that the testing of your faith produces steadfastness. And let steadfastness have its full effect, that you may be perfect and complete, lacking in nothing (James 1:2–4 ESV).

Not only that, but we rejoice in our sufferings, knowing that suffering produces endurance, and endurance produces character, and character produces hope, and hope does not put us to shame, because God's love has been poured into our hearts through the Holy Spirit who has been given to us (Romans 5:3–5 ESV).

Yes, trials and suffering can make it more difficult for us to run the spiritual course set before us—but they don't have to! With God behind us and beside us, suffering can turn into steadfastness. Pain can transform into perseverance. And trials can convert into a blessed hope that can carry us toward the completion of the race that is set before us.

So how will you handle the bumps and bruises you receive in your efforts to follow Christ? Will you allow them to slow you down, or will you use them as fuel for your faithfulness? According to Scripture, the choice is yours.

Determine to React with Radiance

Speaking of choice, it is important that we address our own actions and attitudes when we encounter difficult circumstances. In many ways, how we conduct ourselves throughout our spiritual walk is just as important as finishing the race.

What do I mean by that? Well, I've known some Christians in my day who were high on endurance but low on love. They were determined to persevere amid persecution, but they made sure everyone around them knew how miserable they were. In turn, they made life miserable for many others who happened to encounter them in the middle of their race.

Such an attitude is not befitting for servants of the King of kings. As Christians, we are called not only to run with endurance and finish the race, but to do so in a way that encourages others to follow us. We have been commanded not only to be disciples of Jesus, but to make disciples. For that to happen, we need to reflect the love, grace, and goodness of the Savior that we follow.

When we are confronted by all the ugliness Jesus predicted for the World of the End, we can respond by radiating the love of Christ. We can live, as Paul said in Romans 12:12, "Rejoicing in hope, patient in tribulation, continuing steadfastly in prayer."

Remember Peter's words to the early Christians, "What credit is it if, when you are beaten for your faults, you take it patiently? But when you do good and suffer, if you take it patiently, this is commendable before God. For to this you were called, because Christ also suffered for us, leaving us an example, that you should follow in His steps: 'Who committed no sin, nor was deceit found in His mouth'; who, when He was reviled, did not revile in return; when He suffered, He did not threaten, but committed Himself to Him who judges righteously" (1 Peter 2:20–23).

Developing perseverance as a believer in Jesus does not have to be a bitter experience. Yes, each of us will need to endure unpleasant seasons, but we can use those seasons as opportunities to radiate the love and light of Christ.

Determine to Reach Your Goal

We typically connect the book of Revelation with the chaos and cataclysms we expect to experience at the end of the world. The vision John received on the island of Patmos certainly allows us to peek through the window of time and glimpse many important details about the end of history. As we've seen, those details dovetail perfectly with Jesus' prophecy in the Olivet Discourse.

Yet there's a section of Revelation we sometimes forget. In chapters 2 and 3, the Lord Jesus commissioned John to deliver seven letters to the seven churches operating in Asia Minor during his day. Each of those letters carried a specific message that utilized imagery relevant to those specific regions. Taken together, they create a wonderful word of encouragement and exhortation from Christ to His Church during a season of intense persecution.

There is one specific theme present in each of those letters in Revelation that is pertinent to this chapter. See if you can catch that theme based on the verses below.

- For the church at Ephesus: "To him who overcomes I will give to eat from the tree of life, which is in the midst of the Paradise of God" (2:7).

- For the church at Smyrna: "He who overcomes shall not be hurt by the second death" (2:11).

- For the church at Pergamos: "To him who overcomes I will give some of the hidden manna to eat. And I will give him a white stone, and on the stone a new name written which no one knows except him who receives it" (2:17).

- For the church at Thyatira: "And he who overcomes, and keeps My works until the end, to him I will give power over the nations—'He shall rule them with a rod of iron; they shall be dashed to pieces like the potter's vessels'—as I also have received from My Father; and I will give him the morning star" (2:26–28).

- For the church at Sardis: "He who overcomes shall be clothed in white garments, and I will not blot out his name from the Book of Life" (3:5).

- For the church at Philadelphia: "He who overcomes, I will make him a pillar in the temple of My God, and he shall go out no more. I will write on him the name of My God and the name of the city of My God, the New Jerusalem, which comes down out of heaven from My God. And I will write on him My new name" (3:12).

- For the church at Laodicea: "To him who overcomes I will grant to sit with Me on My throne, as I also overcame and sat down with My Father on His throne" (3:21).

Do you see the pattern? In every church, Jesus called the believers to overcome, to endure. Jesus exhorts them to push past the persecution and the pain they are experiencing. And with every call to overcome, Jesus included a promised reward.

This is the overwhelming message of God's Word. As children of God, our Savior is calling us to be steadfast in taking our stand for His values, His priorities, and His Kingdom. He is calling us to remain faithful even when the going gets tough.

However, He is also encouraging us to receive the rewards He has promised. This begins with eternal life, and if we never received any other gift from the Father, we would be blessed beyond all possible comprehension! But He has promised even more gifts than life eternal. He has promised exceedingly, abundantly more than we can ask or imagine.

So don't give up in your spiritual walk. Don't allow yourself to be knocked off course or taken out of the race. And if you do stumble, get back up and start running again. No matter what happens, just keep going. Because your reward is worth it.

APPLICATION

Personal Questions

1. Read Matthew 24:13.

   a. What does it mean to endure?

   b. Why would Jesus tell His disciples to endure "to the end"?

   c. What would His disciples need to endure?

Gather & Grow

Nature Walk: 5:15pm
Potluck Meal: 6:30pm
Fire & Fellowship: 7:00–9:00pm

Oct 5

The Olson Farm
1645 10th St SE
Buffalo, MN 55313

Diane Olson is hosting a
beautiful nature walk through
the woods and a warm fire
for laughter & fellowship.

Bring a dish to share
and a friend or neighbor!

A Women's Ministry Event
Raining: Meet at Riverwood

d. What does it look like for Christians to endure in today's culture?

2. How do you remind yourself to keep going and endure for Christ when life becomes difficult? What encouragements and promises from the Bible help you to endure spiritually?

3. Read 2 Timothy 2:3, 10.

    a. How did Paul instruct Timothy to endure?

    b. How do these verses encourage you to endure as well?

4. Read Ephesians 6:10–13.

    a. How are we to "stand" against the "wiles of the devil"?

b. What are we to put on?

5. Why does enduring as a follower of Jesus require both strength and stamina?

6. Compare and contrast what salvation is and is not from the section "The Satisfaction of Our Stand."

7. Based on this lesson, explain the three specific ways you can start practicing your endurance as a Christian.

Group Questions

1. Read Matthew 24:13.

   a. What does Jesus command us to endure?

   b. "To the end" of what are we to endure for Him?

2. Read Ephesians 6:10–13.

   a. How are we to be "strong" (see verse 10)?

   b. How are we to withstand the devil's "wiles" (see verse 11)?

c. What are we fighting against (see verse 13)?

d. How can you take a stand for Jesus and endure in today's world?

3. Discuss as a group what the terms *endurance, steadfastness, faithfulness,* and *perseverance* have in common.

4. Why are stamina and strength needed to endure for Christ? What do they help us do?

5. As a group, compare and contrast perennial stamina with personal stamina.

6. Review the sections "What This Salvation Is Not" and "What This Salvation Is."

   a. Does standing for Christ alone erase our sin? Why or why not?

   b. How are we saved according to Ephesians 2:8–9?

   c. Because of salvation in Christ, why are we to expect persecution? Should we be afraid of persecution? Why or why not (2 Timothy 4:18 NIV)?

   d. Describe what salvation is and is not.

7. How do you practice endurance as a Christ follower?

DID YOU KNOW?

Prior to his final trip to Jerusalem, the apostle Paul told a group of Ephesian elders, "And see, now I go bound in the spirit to Jerusalem, not knowing the things that will happen to me there, except that the Holy Spirit testifies in every city, saying that chains and tribulations await me. But none of these things move me; nor do I count my life dear to myself, so that I may finish my race with joy, and the ministry which I received from the Lord Jesus, to testify to the gospel of the grace of God" (Acts 20:22–24). No matter what happens, let's finish our individual races with endurance!

Note
1. Lisa Jhung, "He Ran the Sahara," *Runner's World*, May 8, 2009, https://www.runnersworld.com/runners-stories/a20800083/charlie-engle-of-running-the-sahara/.

LEADER'S GUIDE

Thank you for your commitment to lead a group through *The World of the End*. Being a leader has its own rewards. You may discover that your walk with the Lord deepens through this experience. Throughout the study guide, your group will explore new topics and review study questions that encourage thought-provoking group discussion.

The lessons in this study guide are suitable for Sunday school classes, small-group studies, elective Bible studies, or home Bible study groups. Each lesson is structured to provoke thought and help you grow in your knowledge and understanding of God. There are multiple components in this section that can help you structure your lessons and discussion time, so make sure you read and consider each one.

Before You Begin

Before you begin each meeting, make sure you and your group are well-versed with the content of the lesson. Group members should have their own study guide so they can follow along and write in the study guide if need be. You may wish to assign the study guide lesson as homework prior to the meeting of the group and then use the meeting time to discuss the lesson.

To ensure that everyone has a chance to participate in the discussion, the ideal size for a group is around eight to ten people. If there are more than ten people, try to break up the bigger group into smaller subgroups. Make sure the members are committed to participating each week, as this will help create stability and help you better prepare the structure of the meeting.

At the beginning of the study each week, start the session with a question to challenge group members to think about the issues you will be discussing. The members can answer briefly, but the goal is to have an idea in their mind as you go over the lesson. This allows the group members to become engaged and ready to interact with the group.

After reviewing the lesson, try to initiate a free-flowing discussion. Invite group members to bring questions and insights they may have discovered to the next meeting, especially if they were unsure of the meaning of some parts of the lesson. Be prepared to discuss how biblical truth applies to the world we live in today.

Weekly Preparation

As the group leader, here are a few things you can do to prepare for each meeting:

- *Make sure you are thoroughly familiar with the material in the lesson.* Make sure you understand the content of the lesson so you know how to structure group time and are prepared to lead group discussion.

- *Decide, ahead of time, which questions you want to discuss.* Depending on how much time you have each week, you may not be able to reflect on every question. Select specific questions that you feel will evoke the best discussion.

- *Take prayer requests.* At the end of your discussion, take prayer requests from your group members and pray for each other.

Structuring the Discussion Time

As the group leader, it is up to you to keep track of the time and keep things moving along according to your schedule. If your group is having a good discussion, don't feel the need to stop and move on to the next question. Remember, the purpose is to pull together ideas and share unique insights on the lesson. Make time each week to discuss how to apply these truths to living for Christ today.

The purpose of discussion is for everyone to participate, but don't be concerned if certain group members are more quiet—they may be internally reflecting on the questions and need time to process their ideas before they can share them.

If you need help in organizing your time when planning your group Bible study, the following schedule, for sixty minutes and ninety minutes, can give you a structure for the lesson:

Section	60 Minutes	90 Minutes
WELCOME: Members arrive and get settled	5 minutes	10 minutes
GETTING STARTED QUESTION: Prepares the group for interacting with one another	10 minutes	10 minutes
MESSAGE: Review the lesson	15 minutes	25 minutes
DISCUSSION: Discuss group study questions	25 minutes	35 minutes
PRAYER AND APPLICATION : Final application for the week and prayer before dismissal	5 minutes	10 minutes

Group Dynamics

Leading a group study can be a rewarding experience for you and your group members—but that doesn't mean there won't be challenges. Certain members may feel uncomfortable discussing topics that they consider very personal and might be afraid of being called on. Some members might have disagreements on specific issues. To help prevent these scenarios, consider the following ground rules:

- If someone has a question that may seem off topic, suggest that it is discussed at another time, or ask the group if they are okay with addressing that topic.

- If someone asks a question you don't know the answer to, confess that you don't know and move on. If you feel comfortable, invite other group members to give their opinions or share their comments based on personal experience.

- If you feel like a couple of people are talking much more than others, direct questions to people who may not have shared yet. You could even ask the more dominating members to help draw out the quiet ones.

- When there is a disagreement, encourage the group members to process the matter in love. Invite members from opposing sides to evaluate their opinions and consider the ideas of the other members. Lead the group through Scripture that addresses the topic, and look for common ground.

When issues arise, encourage your group to think of Scripture: "Love one another" (John 13:34), "If it is possible, as far as it depends on you, live at peace with everyone" (Romans 12:18 NIV), and "Be quick to listen, slow to speak and slow to become angry" (James 1:19 NIV).

ABOUT
DR. DAVID JEREMIAH
AND TURNING POINT

Dr. David Jeremiah is the founder of Turning Point, a ministry committed to providing Christians with sound Bible teaching relevant to today's changing times through radio and television broadcasts, audio series, books, and live events. Dr. Jeremiah's common-sense teaching on topics such as family, prayer, worship, angels, and biblical prophecy forms the foundation of Turning Point.

David and his wife, Donna, reside in El Cajon, California, where he serves as the senior pastor of Shadow Mountain Community Church. David and Donna have four children and twelve grandchildren.

In 1982, Dr. Jeremiah brought the same solid teaching to San Diego television that he shares weekly with his congregation. Shortly thereafter, Turning Point expanded its ministry to radio. Dr. Jeremiah's inspiring messages can now be heard worldwide on radio, television, and the Internet.

Because Dr. Jeremiah desires to know his listening audience, he travels nationwide holding ministry rallies and spiritual enrichment conferences that touch the hearts and lives of many people. According to Dr. Jeremiah, "At some point in time, everyone reaches a turning point; and for every person, that moment is unique, an experience to hold onto forever. There's so much changing in today's world that sometimes it's difficult to choose the right path. Turning Point offers people an understanding of God's Word as well as the opportunity to make a difference in their lives."

Dr. Jeremiah has authored numerous books, including *Escape the Coming Night* (Revelation), *The Handwriting on the Wall* (Daniel), *Overcoming Loneliness, Prayer—The Great Adventure, God in You* (Holy Spirit), *When Your World Falls Apart, Slaying the Giants in Your Life, My Heart's Desire, Hope for Today, Captured by Grace, Signs of Life, What in the World Is Going On?, The Coming*

Economic Armageddon, I Never Thought I'd See the Day!, God Loves You: He Always Has—He Always Will, Agents of the Apocalypse, Agents of Babylon, Revealing the Mysteries of Heaven, People Are Asking . . . Is This the End?, A Life Beyond Amazing, Overcomer, Everything You Need, Forward, and *Where Do We Go from Here?.*

stay connected to the teaching of

DR. DAVID JEREMIAH

. . . .

Publishing | Radio | Television | Online

FURTHER YOUR STUDY OF THIS BOOK

· · · · · · · ·

The World of the End Resource Materials

To enhance your study on this important topic, we recommend the correlating audio message album and DVD messages from *The World of the End* series.

Audio Message Album

The material found in this book originated from messages presented by Dr. Jeremiah at Shadow Mountain Community Church where he serves as senior pastor. These nine messages are conveniently packaged in an accessible audio album.

DVD Message Presentations

Watch Dr. Jeremiah deliver *The World of the End* original messages in this special DVD collection.

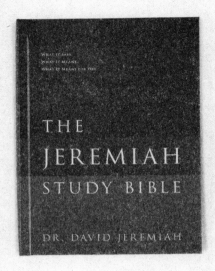

COMPANION BOOK
TO ENRICH YOUR
STUDY EXPERIENCE

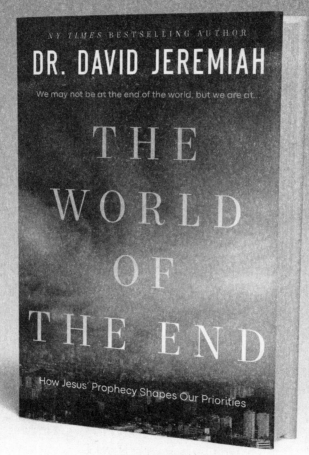

NY TIMES BESTSELLING AUTHOR

DR. DAVID JEREMIAH

We may not be at the end of the world, but we are at...

THE
WORLD
OF
THE END

How Jesus' Prophecy Shapes Our Priorities

ISBN 9780785251996

Available wherever books are sold

W PUBLISHING GROUP

New Bible Study Series
from Dr. David Jeremiah

The Jeremiah Bible Study Series captures Dr. David Jeremiah's forty-plus years of commitment to teaching the whole Word of God. Each volume contains twelve lessons for individuals and groups to explore what the Bible says, what it meant to the people at the time it was written, and what it means to us today. Out of his lifelong ministry of *delivering the unchanging Word of God to an ever-changing world*, Dr. Jeremiah has written this Bible-strong study series focused not on causes, current events, or politics, but on the solid truth of Scripture.

9780310091493	Matthew	9780310091660	Galatians
9780310091516	Mark	9780310091684	Ephesians
9780310091530	Luke	9780310091707	Philippians
9780310091554	John	9780310091721	Colossians and Philemon
9780310091608	Acts	9780310091745	1 and 2 Thessalonians
9780310091622	Romans	9780310091769	1 and 2 Timothy and Titus
9780310091646	1 Corinthians	9780310091806	James
9780310097488	2 Corinthians	9780310091868	Revelation

Available now at your favorite bookstore.

Where Do We Go From Here?

The more we look around today, the more it seems our world is hanging by a thread. We're emerging from the pangs of a pandemic, the economy is in flux, the church is in decline, and Jerusalem once again sits atop the powder keg of global politics.

These colliding crises in our culture are not random misfortunes but are as connected as a spider's web. With each passing day, forces are pushing us closer to the end of history. Yet this is not a time for despair! Instead, it is a time to examine the assurance of God's prophetic plan.

In this book and study guide, bestselling author Dr. David Jeremiah will help you do just that by exploring ten current moments and movements in light of that plan. Each chapter highlights what's happening, what Scripture says, and where we can go from here. In the end, you'll be reminded once again that our exalted Lord, the risen Christ, knows the way forward!

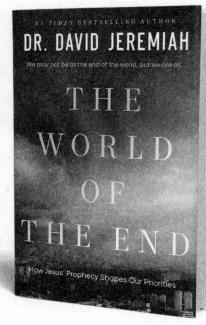
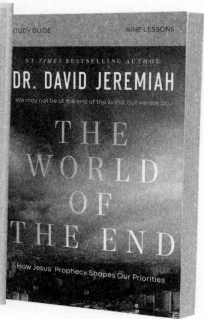

Hardcover
9780785251996

Bible Study Guide
9780310155928

Available now at your favorite bookstore.

 Harper*Christian* Resources

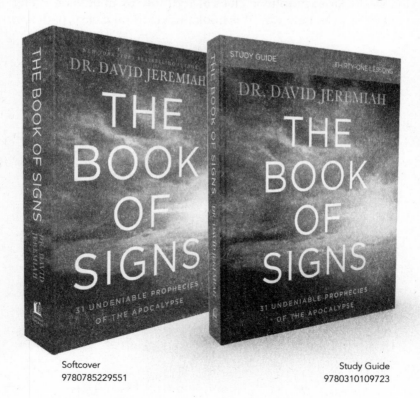

STAY CONNECTED TO DAVID JEREMIAH

• • • • • • • •

Take advantage of three great ways to let Dr. David Jeremiah
give you spiritual direction every day!

Turning Points Magazine and Devotional

Receive Dr. Jeremiah's magazine,
Turning Points, each month:
- Thematic study focus
- 52 pages of life-changing reading
- Relevant articles
- Daily devotional readings and more!

Request *Turning Points* magazine today!
(800) 947-1993 | <u>DavidJeremiah.org/Magazine</u>

Daily Turning Point E-Devotional

Receive a daily e-devotion from Dr. Jeremiah
that will strengthen your walk with God and
encourage you to live the authentic Christian life.

Sign up for your free e-devotional today!
<u>www.DavidJeremiah.org/Devo</u>

Turning Point Mobile App

Access Dr. Jeremiah's video teachings,
audio sermons, and more . . . whenever and
wherever you are!

Download your free app today!
<u>www.DavidJeremiah.org/App</u>